ISBN: 979-8-9852859-0-1 (print only).

Book Design by Roberta Morris, Leave It to 'Berta.

Cover art: *En Medio del Pueblo* (In the Middle of the Village), Fernando Llort, 2002. Fernando Llort Foundation.

Photographs of the art of Fernando Llort provided by the Fundación Fernando Llort, San Salvador, El Salvador. Juan Pablo Llort, President.

Map image © iStock/bgblue

Published by Story Tree Prints, Great Falls, VA, 2022.

For more information, email ahrensted@gmail.com.

PAINTING JOY:
THE ART AND LIFE OF FERNANDO LLORT

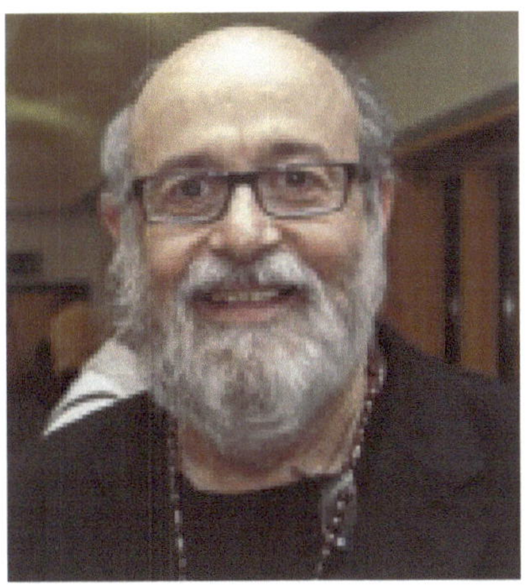

Fernando Llort Choussy

(1949-2018)

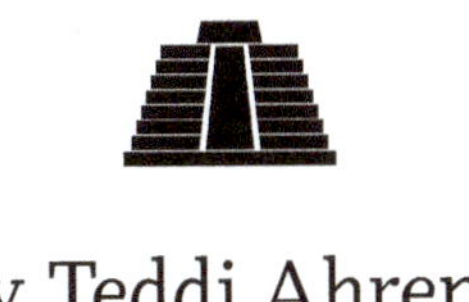

by Teddi Ahrens

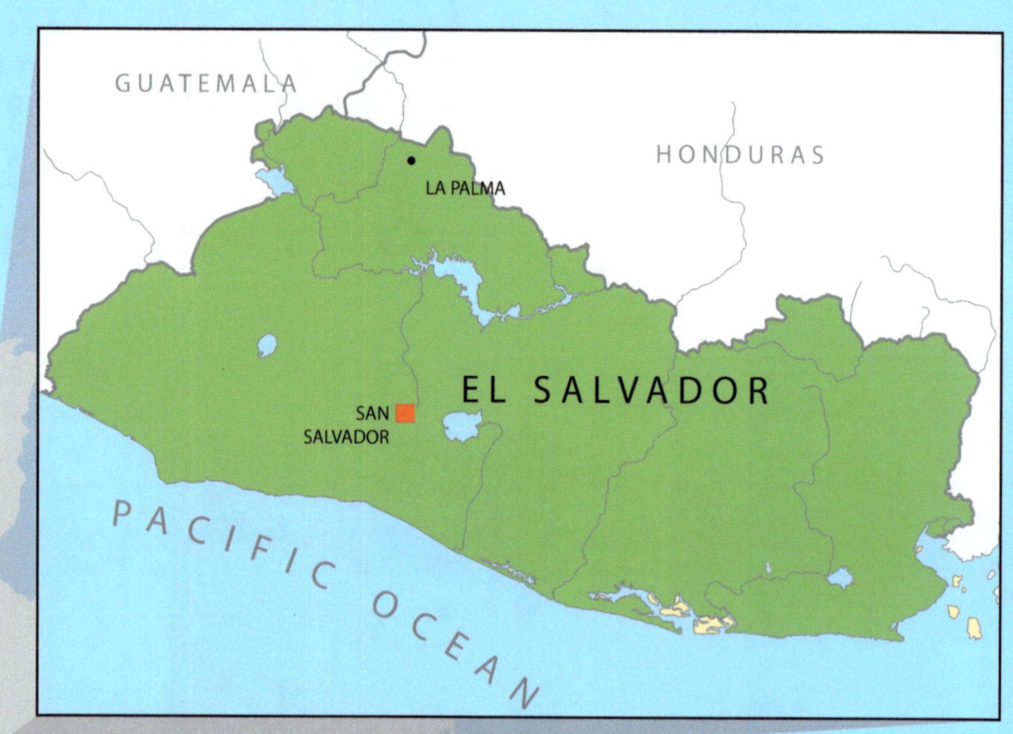

GUATEMALA
HONDURAS
LA PALMA
EL SALVADOR
SAN SALVADOR
PACIFIC OCEAN

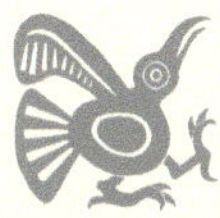

ACKNOWLEDGEMENTS

BEFORE I MET FERNANDO LLORT, I was already awed by his paintings and how he had transformed the village of La Palma. I wanted to tell the world about him and his belief in the power of art. He welcomed my questions, agreed to my writing his story, and said farewell with a warm hug. I owe special gratitude to his son Juan Pablo, his daughter María José, his beloved wife Estela, his sister, cousin, and many friends who trusted me with their memories and stories: I couldn't have written this book without their support.

Thanks to my friend Archer Heinzen and companions for my first trip to El Salvador with Co-Partners of *Campesinas* in 2012. I returned another six times because I fell in love with the Salvadoran people and their country. Many thanks to Julie Williams, my traveling friend who came with me, and who has supported me in so many ways.

I owe much appreciation to my writers group, Terry Jennings, Judith Tabler, and Kim Waxman, who coped with many, many drafts of the original manuscript.

To my dear friend Ellen McFarland who has always been there helping me brainstorm, recover from computer disasters, and giving me countless hours of reading, editing and encouragement. My love and gratitude.

To the people of Highlights Foundation, my thanks for the inspiring faculty, especially Nancy Werlin, Sarah Aronson, and Leda Schubert, and workshops that made all the difference.

In memory of Sister Celestine FSPA, whose exuberant teaching and notes on my college essays encouraged me to keep writing.

And to my husband Tom, and to Joe, Mike and Kate, my love and gratitude for your patience and good humor, joining me in my pursuit of adventure, and for your support of the writing those travels inspired.

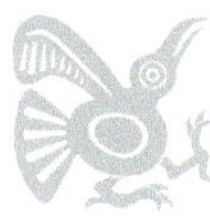

TABLE OF CONTENTS

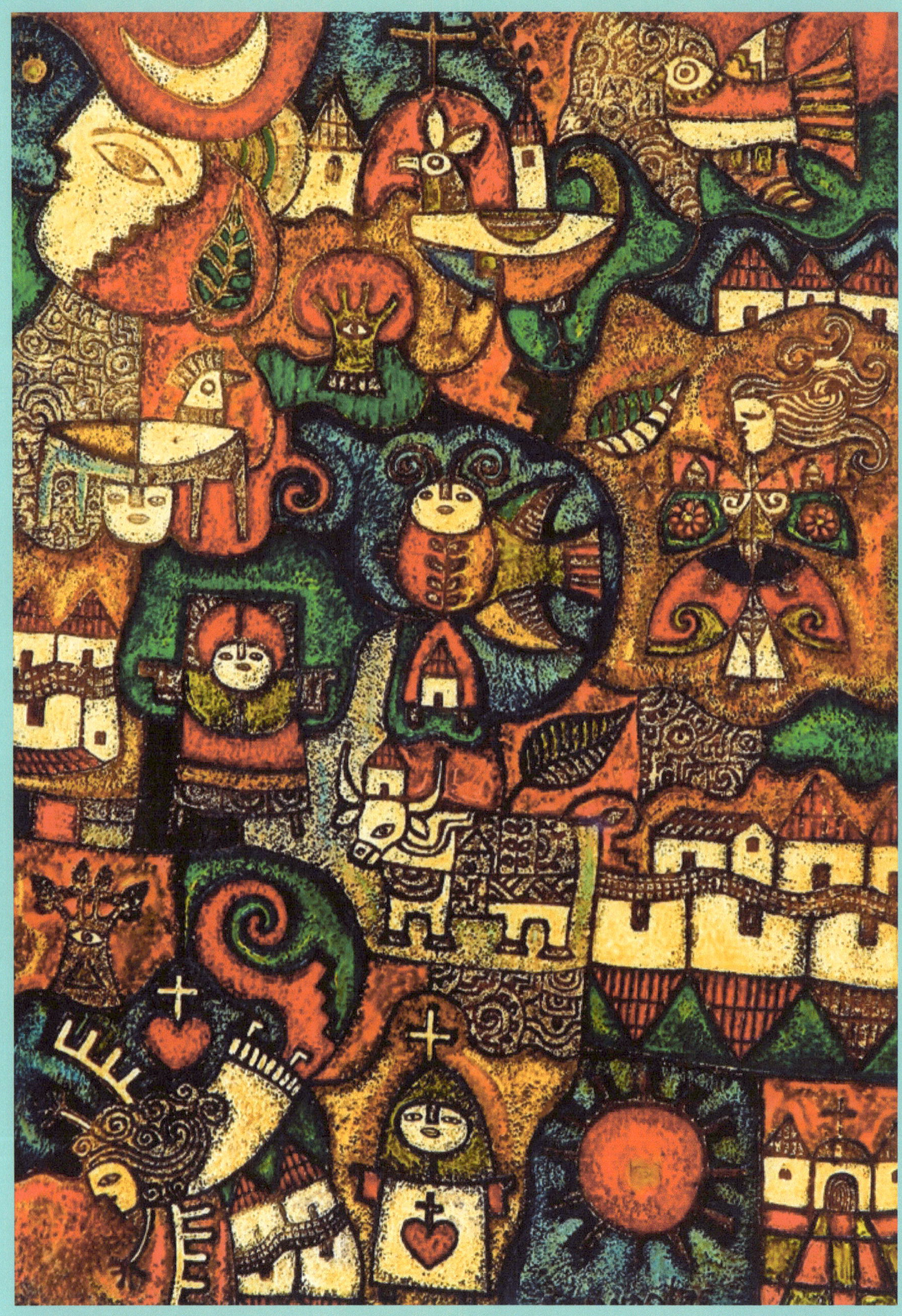

1. *Colores* (Colors), Fernando Llort, 1980. Fernando Llort Foundation.

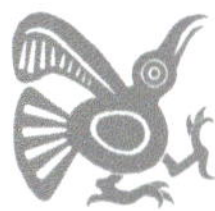

BEGINNINGS

FOR AS LONG AS HE COULD REMEMBER, Fernando Llort (pronounced "yort") loved drawing. When he was a boy, he drew the pictures he imagined on scraps of paper, and when he played outdoors, he sculpted the clay into hills or houses, or animals. But he never imagined that one day his drawings would change the fate of a village and restore a sense of identity for the people of his country.

Fernando created his designs by stirring together a bit of fantasy with symbols used by the Mayan ancestors of modern-day Salvadorans. *Colores* (fig. 1) portrays a landscape with houses along cobblestone roads, plants and animals. People are costumed in unusual dress, including what looks like a helmeted *Conquistador* and a Mayan with his headdress and collar. Mayan art and designs adorn the bull and open spaces. The people of El Salvador recognized themselves and their countryside in these images. The images also awakened them to their ancient roots and pride in their cultural heritage. Fernando became their beloved national artist.

Fernando Llort Choussy was born on April 7, 1949, the fourth of six children, in San Salvador, the largest city and capital of El Salvador. His mother was Francia Victoria Choussy, and his father was Baltasar Llort Escalante. Fernando was raised a Catholic, and his childhood was a happy mix of play and mischief with his sister, four brothers, and their German Shepherd dog and parrot. And he always loved to draw.

As a young man, his father helped search for survivors of the devastating 1951 Jucuapa earthquake not far from San Salvador. Deeply moved by the experience, he founded the Volunteer Rescue Corps of the Salvadoran Red Cross and became a dedicated humanitarian. Both parents taught the children by their example to honor the dignity of all people and to help anyone they saw who was in trouble.[1]

During the holidays and long, hot summers, the Llort family spent weeks in La Palma, a small village nestled in the mountains about two hours north of their home in San Salvador. Their cottage, like many others in La Palma, had no electricity or indoor plumbing, but it was surrounded by beauty and cooled by mountain breezes. And there was plenty of space for Fernando and his siblings to play and explore. They swam in the stream, roamed the forest, caught snakes and molded shapes with the clay soil. Fernando soon discovered he could sculpt figures of clay as well. La Palma would always be his favorite place in the world.[2]

When summer ended one year, Fernando didn't want to be left home when his siblings were going off to school. He cried and begged his parents to let him go too. Although he was only four years old, they persuaded the school director to admit him to first grade. Fernando was even more delighted when he realized that school meant access to paper and notebooks, and he couldn't resist drawing instead of paying attention in class. Seeing the maps he created, his geography teacher invited Fernando to use the blackboard and show the other children how to do it.

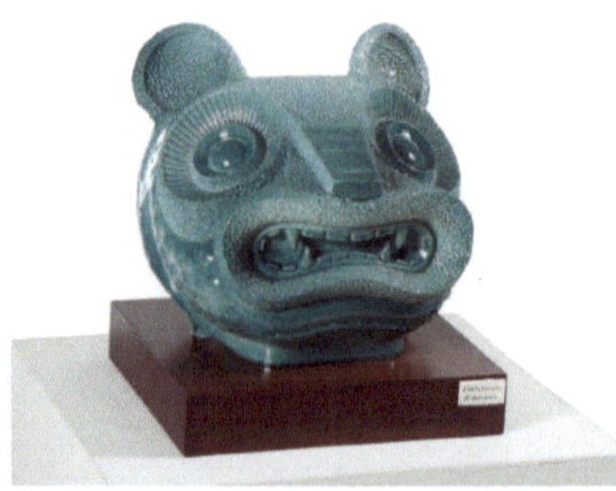

2. Jaguar sculpture, César Sermeño, 1986. Museum of Art of El Salvador. Free use photo.

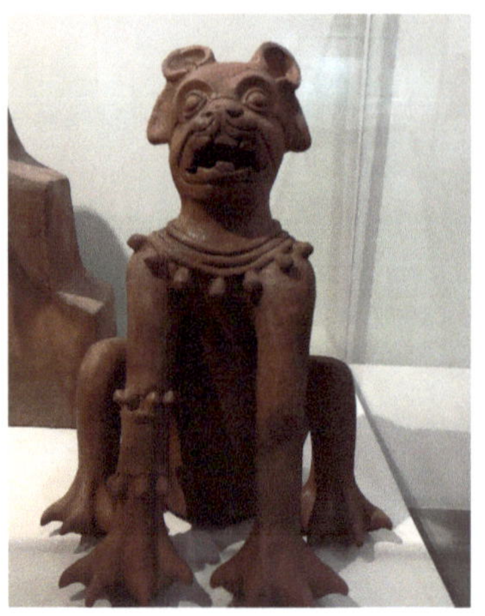

3. Jaguar sculpture, Cihuatan archeological site, AD 900-1,250. National Museum of Anthropology, San Salvador. Free use photo.

Dilemmas

Because he had started school so young, Fernando was only 15 years old when he graduated from high school in October 1964. After graduation, young people were expected to enroll in college, take vocational courses, or start working. Fernando was already most interested in art and painting, and he didn't want to do anything else. His father expected him to continue his education like his older brothers - but in architecture, not art. It was Fernando's duty to respect his father's decisions, so he applied to the School of Architecture at the University of El Salvador and was accepted. His classes wouldn't begin until spring, so Fernando was able to study art during the months in between.

He enrolled in classes with Master César Sermeño, a renowned artist and ceramic sculptor, among the few Salvadoran artists portraying authentic symbols of Central America, not those of Europe. At the time, Sermeño taught classes in design, modeling and ceramics at the Department of Plastic Arts[3] of the General Directorate of Fine Arts in San Salvador.[4]

Described as the "poet of clay," Sermeño's stylized plants and animals echoed elements found in remains of art dating back to early Mayan culture. For example, his sculpture of the fierce jaguar in figure 2 resembles the jaguar in figure 3 found at an ancient Central American site. In Mayan cosmology, the jaguar is a powerful god who can pass between the world of the living and the world of the ancestors. Sermeño added dimension and detail to his creations by cutting lines into the clay (note the detail around each eye of the jaguar), just as the Mayans did to decorate their ceramics (figs. 4, 5).[5]

This ceramics course was Fernando's only formal art instruction, and the experience made a lasting impression on him. Taking lessons from a master, he learned techniques of molding and sculpting clay and carving designs in it. Sermeño praised and encouraged him, telling him to "follow his passion."[6] When the course ended, Fernando told his father again that he wanted to be an artist.

"No," his father said, "Art is a hobby, not a career."[7]

Fernando was disappointed, but he obeyed his father. He began his studies in the school of architecture that spring as planned, but he wasn't happy. In his mind, architecture had too many rules. It didn't allow for the imaginative drawing he wanted to do. But if he couldn't be an artist, he worried, what else would be fulfilling?

He wanted to do something worthwhile, where he could make a difference for others. Not just have a career and make money. With these thoughts in mind, Fernando joined other students on a spiritual retreat, and he was inspired to become a priest. This time, his parents were overjoyed. Of all vocations, the priesthood was the highest, most respected role that a Catholic youth could hope for.

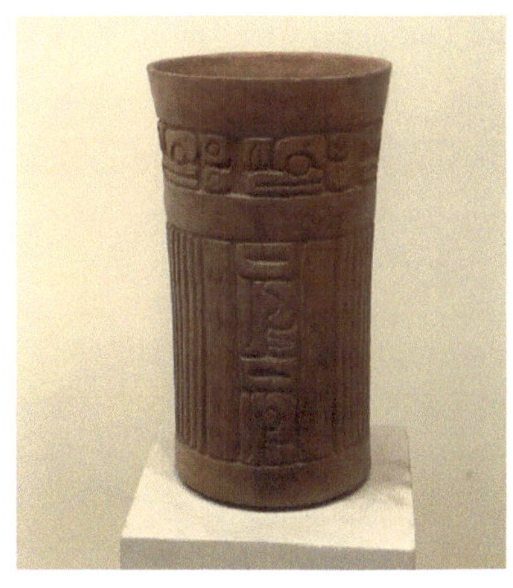

4. Pre-Columbian vase, AD 600-900. National Museum of Anthropology, San Salvador. Free use photo.

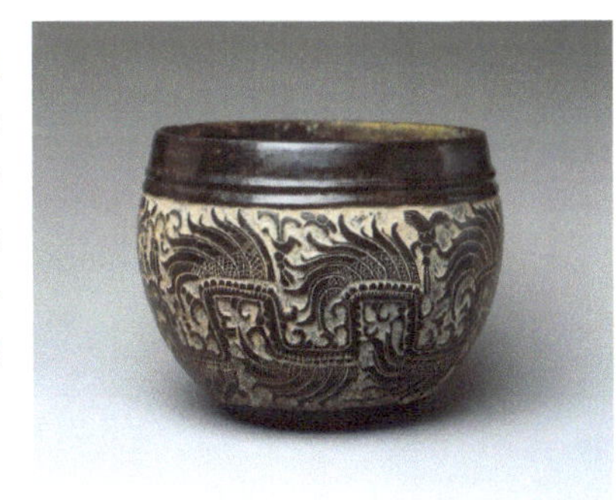

5. Pre-Columbian bowl, AD 539. Metropolitan Museum of Art, New York, NY. Free use photo.

Fernando in Europe

Fernando was sixteen years old when he entered the seminary in Columbia. The next year, in 1966, he studied philosophy in Toulouse, France, and then theology in Belgium, but he still hungered for art. Fortunately, he was not far from some of the biggest art museums in the world. He had never gazed at such a collection of masterpieces, and he couldn't resist seeing as much as possible.

During those three years in Europe, he visited all the major museums, including the Louvre and Musée d'Orsay in Paris, the Rijksmuseum in Amsterdam, the Prado in Madrid, the Uffizi in Florence, and the Vatican Museum in Rome.[8] In each museum, he paid attention to the artists' subjects, the techniques, even their brush strokes. He was awed and inspired by what he saw.

Fernando paid special attention to the styles and techniques of the twentieth century artists he admired. The abstract, layered images of Picasso's art fascinated him. As his own style evolved, Fernando also experimented with bold outlines and abstract figures in the style of Henri Matisse and Joan Miró (fig. 6). But his images were always of the people and natural environment of El Salvador, and his colors bright and fantastical.

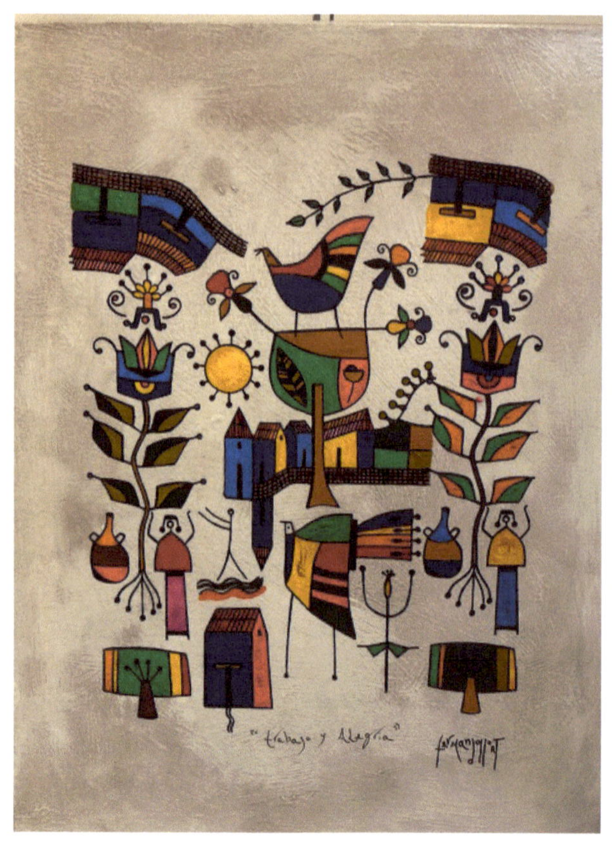

6. *Trabajo y Alegría* (Work and Happiness), Fernando Llort, 1996. Private collection.

Seeing his interest in European art, his seminary classmates in Toulouse asked him about the art and culture of El Salvador. Fernando struggled to answer them because his country's cultural heritage is both complicated and tragic.

El Salvador is the smallest country in Central America, about the size of Massachusetts. Thousands of years ago, the Mayan people inhabited its entire western region, living in a few dozen city-states. They developed a sophisticated culture, noted for its architecture, mathematics, calendar and a writing system. Well-preserved pyramids and temples still stand which tell of the many gods they worshipped. Symbols represent the gods of creation and abundance, the god of thunder and the god of darkness, to name a few.

A major portion of the Mayan Empire was buried under the ashes of a "mega-eruption" of the Ilopango volcano, near what is now San Salvador. Radio-carbon tests date the event to AD 431.[9] The destruction and ash spread as much as 80 kilometers (49.7 miles) outward, leaving the land uninhabitable for several decades. The Mayan people continued to live in city-states not affected by the volcano, but only for a few more centuries. Explanations for why they disappeared range from extreme draught and environmental disaster to societal breakdown, but by AD 900, all the city-states had been abandoned. Small agricultural villages remained, and they clung to their language and many of their old ways.

Then another disaster struck in the 1500s when the Spanish invaded. As they did in neighboring countries, the *Conquistadores* (fig. 7) enslaved the people and outlawed their native cultures, languages, and traditions. Ninety percent of the indigenous population died because of bloodshed and infectious diseases.[10]

The survivors had no choice but to adopt the foreign culture of the invaders. They were forced to speak Spanish and forbidden to wear their traditional dress, and they were converted to Catholicism. Soon, no one could remember when it had been any different. Only excavated ruins of

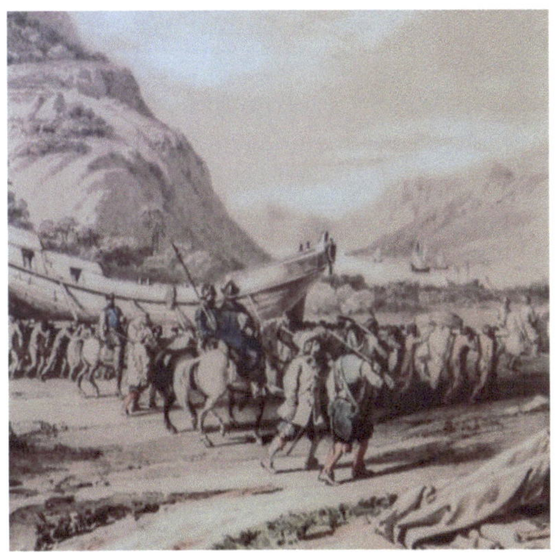

7. Portrayal of the Conquistadors by unknown artist. *Exploradores* Visitors Centre, Trujillo, Spain. Free use photo.

their temples and burial sites, clay remnants of statues and urns, and pockets of native languages are left of those early cultures. Modern Salvadorans could not look to the past to say who they were. Their roots, their link to the past had been destroyed.

Fernando told his seminary classmates that he couldn't show them any paintings "to highlight the legends, the stories, and the figures that shaped my country."[11] He pointed out that European artists portrayed their own cultures, their own heroes and myths and history. Not only was there no Central American art to speak of in European museums, there were few opportunities to see Salvadoran art even in his own country. No one established an art museum in El Salvador until Julia Díaz did so years later, in 1983. The talented artists of El Salvador such as Salarrué, Carlos Cañas, Armando Solís, and Julia Díaz painted pre-Columbian portrayals of El Salvador. However, they often studied in Europe and the United States and supported themselves by teaching or exhibiting there more than at home. So Fernando decided to create paintings of El Salvador himself.

While he continued his studies for the priesthood, Fernando sketched and painted in his free time. By the time he graduated with a degree in philosophy in the spring of 1969, he had completed 22 paintings. A friend was so impressed that he arranged for an exhibit in Toulouse. Admirers were drawn to his vivid colors and unique portrayals of the Salvadoran countryside, and they purchased every single painting. When he told this story years later, Fernando still expressed his surprise and delight about the success of that first exhibit.[12]

The next year, he began his theology studies in Belgium, the second step toward the priesthood. After almost three years away, Fernando missed his family and the warmth and brightness of the Salvadoran climate. Northern Europe began to seem cold and dreary, but he realized that it was not only the climate that was bothering him. He was in the wrong place, but more than that, he was pursuing the wrong vocation. Art was his vocation, not the priesthood.

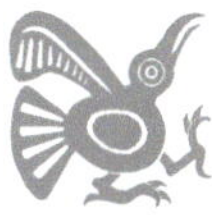

BACK HOME IN EL SALVADOR

NOW 20 YEARS OLD, FERNANDO RETURNED HOME and told his parents again that he was meant to be an artist. No one knows for sure what else he said, but his father was still not persuaded. He sent Fernando to Louisiana in the United States to study architecture again and to learn English. Fernando obeyed, but he was miserable. He felt stifled by the rigid rules of architecture, and he was disgusted by the racial prejudice he saw in the United States. Going there was a big mistake.

> *"I went to classes for two months, and that was it,"* Fernando said. *"One day, my roommate [who was also Salvadoran] said, 'I'm going home,' and I said, 'I'm going with you.'"* [13]

A World in Turmoil

At this time, the late 1960s, Fernando was struggling to determine his own future. The world around him seemed to be doing the same thing. From East to West, cities seethed with protests and demonstrations. In the United States, years of civil rights marches had been followed by marches protesting the war in Vietnam. From Paris to Prague, students and workers united to fight "the establishment," that is, people in power, whether in government or business. Protesters piled up street signs, overturned cars, even trees and sidewalk grates, to block streets. They called on citizens to join them—to go on strike for justice and equality. In fact, noting the turmoil, journalists referred to 1968 as the "year of the barricade."[14]

Another movement of young people was growing around the world. These young people, called "hippies," also wanted to create a more just society. They rejected capitalism because it bred inequality. Instead, they sought to spread the message of peace and love.

In San Salvador as elsewhere, the voices urging people to rise up against government corruption and its suppression of protest often came from students. As they did in New York and Rome and other cities, young people filled the streets, demanding reforms, such as restoring land ownership that had been taken from small farmers, better wages for workers, and an end to government human rights violations.

When Fernando came home in 1969, he reunited with friends who yearned to bring justice and harmony to the world. They adopted the "peace and love" philosophy of the hippies, but they didn't feel that street protests would change anything. Like other hippies, they grew their hair long and wore colorful, tie-dyed clothes. And like many young people at that time, they were fans of the Beatles and other popular rock musicians, breaking away from the music of their parents' generation.[15]

Fernando's parents understood his idealism, but as the months passed, they grew concerned about his lack of direction. It was time for him to be practical, they reminded him, to find a useful occupation, to get serious about life. Fernando responded that he had formed a rock band with some friends, *La Banda del Sol* (The Band of the Sun). Now Fernando was busy day and night. He worked on collage and paintings all day, and he earned money as the lead singer and guitarist in band performances several nights a week (fig. 8).

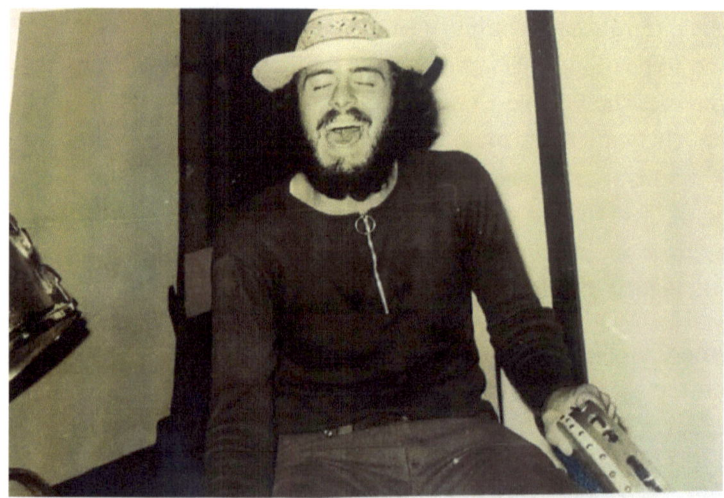

8. Fernando Llort, lead singer in *La Banda del Sol*, 1970.
Llort family photo collection.

La Banda del Sol performed and recorded their songs and became one of the most popular bands in Central America. Although their music was usually about love and reconciliation and peace, the lyrics of one song, "El Planeta de los Cerdos" ("Planet of the Pigs"), insulted government leaders.[16] Officials banned that song on the radio, and one day the police came to the band's rehearsal space and arrested the band members who were there. They jailed them as a warning to other young people. Fernando arrived late, and when he heard what had happened, he turned himself in to join his friends in jail. But the police refused to arrest him.

When he wasn't rehearsing with the band, Fernando spent his time experimenting with his art, trying out different techniques, different media, and composition. He completed enough work to participate in three major art exhibits. He was especially proud of his invitation to *Galería Forma.* Founded by Julia Díaz in 1958, the *Forma* was the only place at that time where visual artists of San Salvador could exhibit their work.[17] Díaz also hosted *La Banda* and other rock concerts in its open space.

Looking back at those years, Fernando did not focus on the turmoil in the world or the dangers young people faced with their dissent. His enduring memories centered around his close friendships, his experiments with art, and the fun and excitement of performing with the band. He said they were among the happiest times in his life.[18]

The Expressive Power of Collage

While Fernando was exploring the museums in Europe, he was struck by the work of Picasso and Matisse. Both artists were known for collage, an art form in which the artist glues together layers of everyday materials, such as fabric, paper, metal, even wood pieces. Although collage originated as an art form in Asia before the 12th century, it became popular in the 1900s when young artists in western Europe and the Americas began to experiment with abstract art and Expressionism. This technique became a way for an artist to give powerful social commentary.

Collage became one of Fernando's favorite techniques.[19] While he continued to sing about peace and love in his band, Fernando felt free to express his personal rebellion against materialism and war in his art (figs. 9, 10, 11).

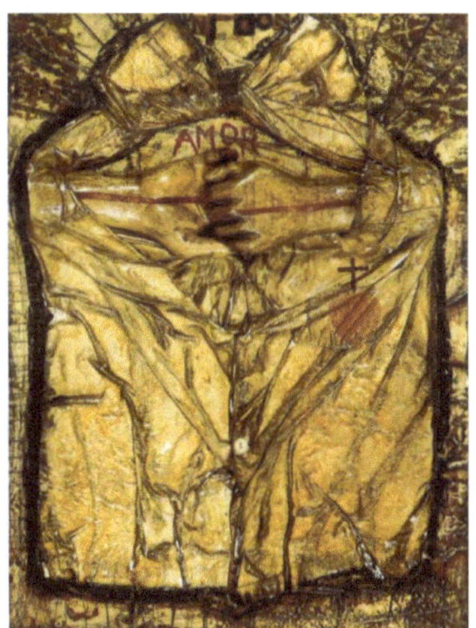

9. *Unidos en Amor* (United in Love), Fernando Llort, 1970. Fernando Llort Foundation.

The collage in figure 9, *Unidos en Amor* (United in Love), depicts hands emerging from what appears to be a shirt with a button on it. There is a cross and an image that might represent a heart. The title itself clarifies both the theme and symbolism of the collage: clasped hands and the red heart represent love, and even the detail of the button makes sense: it's another symbol of holding things together. There is also a red line on each hand and perhaps a butterfly beneath them; Fernando leaves us to ponder what their connection is to the theme.

In the collage in figure 10, titled *Sol,* Fernando used wood and found objects to express his theme. Like a sun, the purple ring hovers over the other elements. Beneath the ring are pieces of wood in the form of a cross and painted images which represent people, some with arms raised in praise. Symbols in this collage also have Mayan roots. For example, the cross is both a Christian and a Mayan symbol. Its four points represent the directions of the wind, the four "opposite" energies which sustain the earth: the dawn, darkness, water and air. The nested rings below may also represent the sun god, which radiates energy that keeps the universe in motion. What appears at first glance to be a random collection of objects becomes a declaration about faith and community.

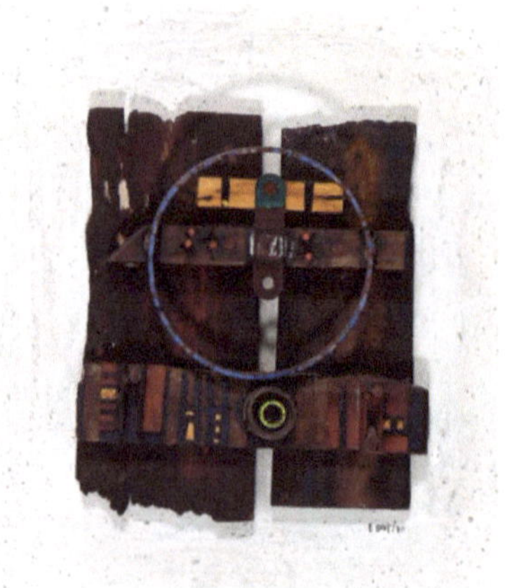

10. *Sol* (Sun), Fernando Llort, 1970. Fernando Llort Foundation.

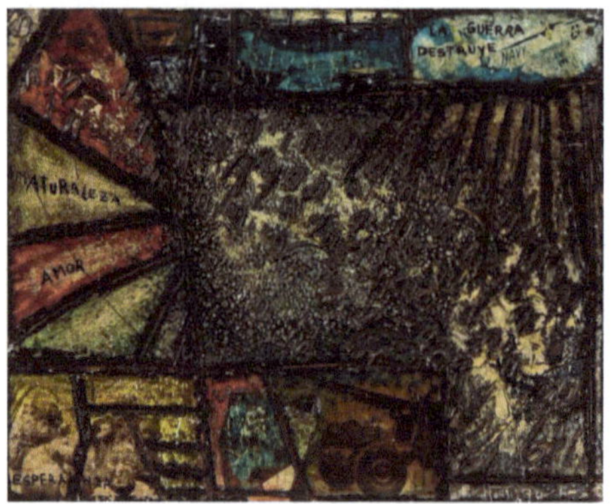

11. *Guerra Con Honduras* (War With Honduras), Fernando Llort, 1970. Private collection.

The collage in figure 11, *Guerra Con Honduras* (War With Honduras), characterizes El Salvador's war with its neighbor as a terrible garden planted with skulls and divided into sections. Map and newspaper cuttings display machines of war and warnings about what is being destroyed.

Throughout his entire life, Fernando Llort was a man of peace and compassion. He abhorred violence, and in early collages like *Guerra Con Honduras*, his feeling of horror is clear. The composition seems to be deliberately out of balance, and the dark images portray weapons, death and despair. This is a sharp contrast to the joyful, vivid symbols which characterize most of his paintings.

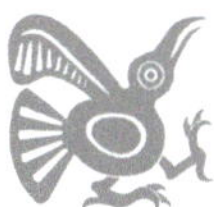

THE TURNING POINT: LA PALMA AND THE COPINOL SEED

FOR SEVERAL MONTHS, FERNANDO LIVED WITH HIS FAMILY IN SAN SALVADOR. He wrote music with his friends and performed with his band all over the city. His parents worried that he was lost and confused, but Fernando had actually found himself. Every day, he surrendered to his imagination and idealism, and he clung to his faith that art had purpose and his talent was a gift that he must not waste. He expressed all of this in his song lyrics, his poetry, and his painting.

He and his bandmates had talked about moving to the countryside to form a commune—to live together like brothers, writing poetry and music and seeking spiritual goods rather than material goods. By the end of 1971, Fernando was ready to leave his family and the city, and he already knew where he would go: to La Palma, the mountain village he had loved since childhood. It turned out that he was the only one of his friends ready to leave at that moment.

The band played their last concert in December 1971. In January, Fernando packed up his paints, his guitar and clothes. He said farewell to his family, and rode the bus up the winding mountain road to La Palma. With his savings from the concerts, he rented a small cabin. At last, he knew he was in the right place. And he knew he would paint. But that's all he knew for sure.

One morning, as Fernando walked down the hill to the market to buy what he needed that day, he noticed a boy crouched under the shade of a copinol tree, working on something with his hands. Curious, he leaned over and saw that the boy had cut and scraped away the shell of a copinol seed. The outer shell was dark brown and about two inches long, and inside was a creamy white center. In Fernando's eyes, it was a perfect frame for a miniature work of art (fig. 12). And his inspiration for the path ahead.[20]

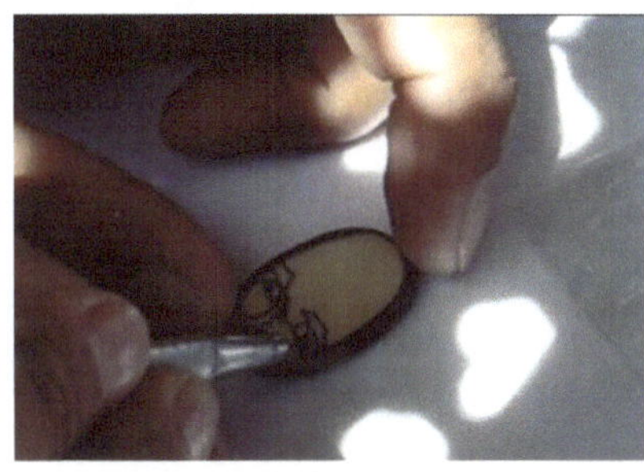

12. Fernando drawing on the center of a copinol seed. Llort family photo collection.

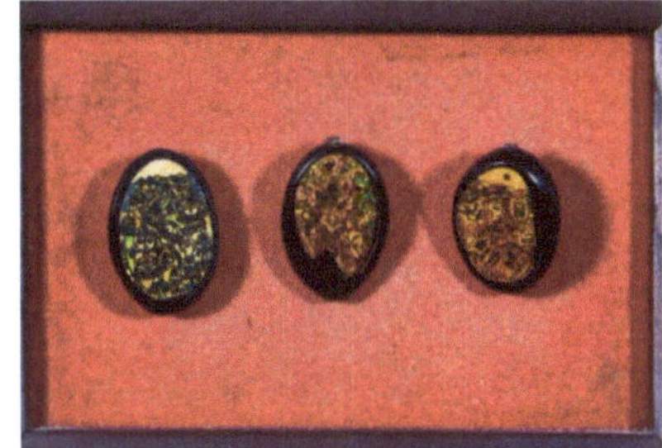

13. *Primeras Semillas* (First Seeds). The first pendants that Fernando made from copinol seeds, 1973. Llort family photo collection.

He collected some seeds, laid them out on his table at the cottage, and cut them in half. Then he spread out his ink markers and colored the interior surface with tiny birds and trees, *casitas* (houses) and corn stalks. Finally, he turned these "seed paintings" into pendants and wore them around his neck (fig. 13).

Fernando sold pendants to some visitors in the village, but he realized he needed to find a market in the city to earn an income. He made more pendants and painted scenes on wooden plaques and brought them to San Salvador. Bringing his work to a few shops, he persuaded them to sell what they could.

Fernando's tiny paintings depicted symbols of the beauty of his country, its creatures, and its people. Customers in the shops bought every piece, and when they found out where he lived, they came to La Palma with friends to buy more.

Several weeks after Fernando moved to La Palma, his friends Julio Medrano, Max Martínez, and Carlos Aragón (known as Tamba) joined him and helped in the workshops. Two bandmates, Óscar Soles and Pedro Portillo, were also painters. They pitched in and shared their skills as well. Seeing more hippies, the villagers stared at their long hair and "funny clothes" (fig. 14), but as time passed, they got used to the newcomers.

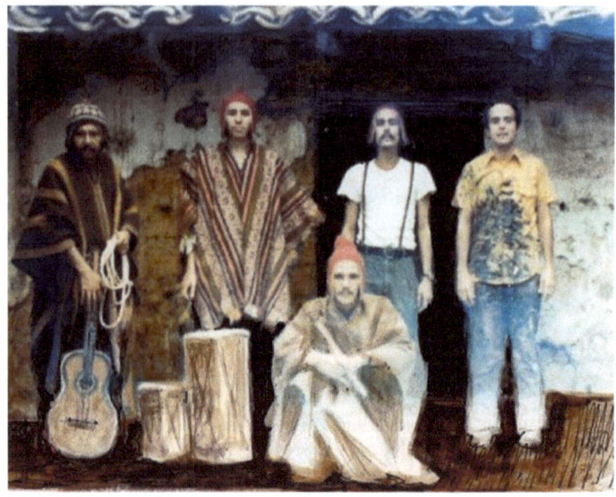

14. Fernando (on right) with some of his friends from the band in La Palma, 1972. Llort family photo collection.

Meeting Estela

Every day, Fernando passed by a house where a beautiful young woman often sat on the porch. He greeted her each day, and she always smiled in return. He wanted to stop and talk to her, but he'd been taught that he had to be properly introduced. Fernando finally met her at the local harvest celebration. Her name was Estela Chacón, and he fell in love with her right then and there.[21] A few months later, she became his wife and partner (fig. 15). Fernando's parents joined the couple in La Palma to celebrate their marriage and gave them the Llort holiday house for their home.

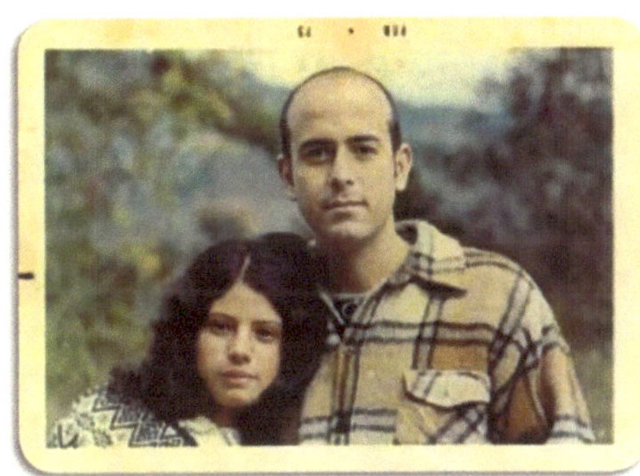

15. Estela and Fernando Llort, 1973.
Llort family photo collection.

When villagers asked Fernando if he would teach them how to make pendants and paint them to sell like he did, he invited them to follow him home. Estela helped organize the workshops that followed.

In the early lessons, Fernando showed the villagers how to cut the copinol seeds and how to paint them using the simple templates he had designed (fig. 16). Members of Estela's family were among Fernando's first students, and Estela worked alongside him. Soon, the art workshops became more and more central to village life.

At last, Fernando had found the meaningful life he had sought and a loving wife to share it. In the next few years, three children, Juan Pablo, María José, and Ángel Fernando, were born. In the evenings when the kids were young, Fernando often took up his guitar and sang to them, and his made-up games sparked their giggles.

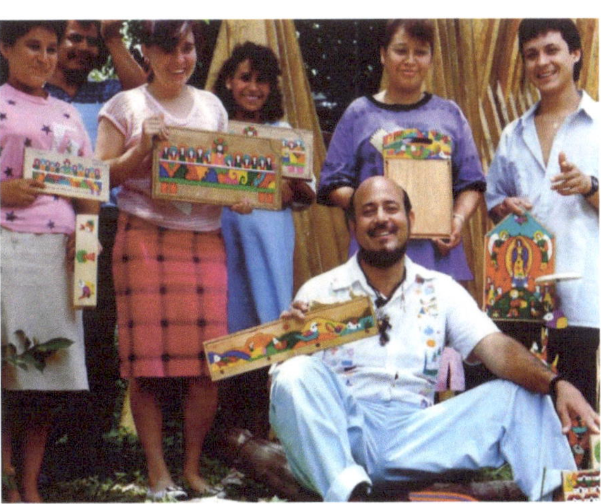

16. Fernando posing with young people of La Palma, now skilled artists and painters, ready to market their wooden crafts. Llort family photo collection.

María José described her childhood as "surrounded by colors, music and the smell of wood and sawdust."[22] Enjoying the freedom and simplicity of life in the countryside and the steadfast love of their parents, the children thrived.

Word soon spread that Fernando was showing people a way to paint and to earn money. Within weeks, he had to find a larger place for his workshops because almost 60 villagers were coming to learn from him. He didn't charge his students anything for the lessons because his students didn't have money to pay him. Fernando hoped he could live on whatever income he earned from sales of his own art in the city. Soon, the inexpensive crafts of the La Palma artists were also popular among the mountain villages and in San Salvador shops.

Fernando was frequently asked how the La Palma workshops began. He would always say that they began with a little boy and a copinol seed.[23]

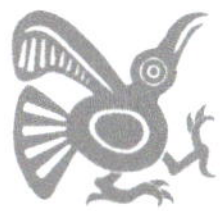

ART LESSONS

"ART MUST BE FREE OF RULES," FERNANDO TOLD HIS STUDENTS, urging them not to feel trapped by what things "really" looked like, nor limit their choice of materials.[24] The deer and armadillos, vines of mandevilla and mango trees in his paintings were familiar to the villagers. Fernando showed them how to exaggerate each image with strong lines and vivid colors. Following his example, the villagers learned to draw figures that represented their everyday lives—their houses, crops, animals, and their faith and traditions.

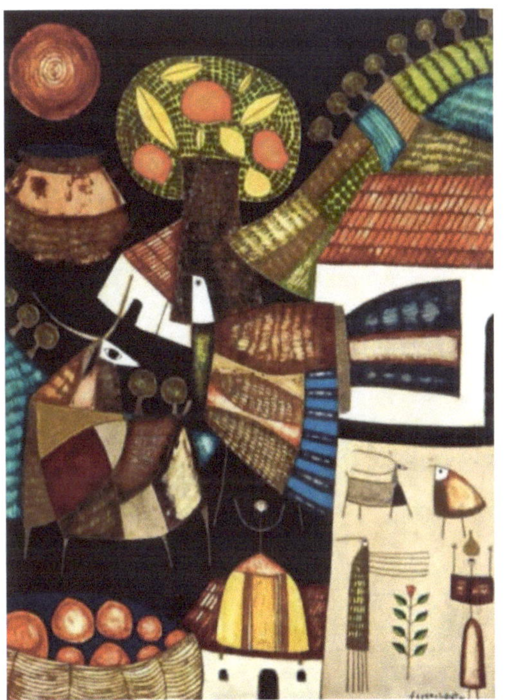

17. *Mi Pueblo y Mi Sueño Mágico*
(My Town and My Magic Dream),
Fernando Llort, 1981.
Fernando Llort Foundation.

Some art critics describe this style of art as naïve or folk art,[25] not creative art, because of its simplicity and portrayal of everyday images. However, folk art is also creative art when its design shows imagination, creative skills and techniques. Fernando's paintings incorporate elements of surrealism, abstract imagery and fanciful designs as he portrays his idealistic vision of El Salvador. For example, tile-roofed houses may be sideways along a road; oversized, angular birds or deer might appear unexpectedly in the foreground of a painting; and a single cornstalk may represent crops and farm work (fig. 17).[26]

Every image had meaning for Fernando. The bird is a sign of peace and the spirit of creation. Many compositions feature eyes scattered among other images, representing the eye of God. The house, *la casita*, is a symbol of the community, and trees are symbols of abundance. He painted hands lifted upward to represent thanksgiving, love and hope. Women are portrayed with almond-shaped eyes, echoing the beauty of their native ancestors. Flowery vines and fruit abound as symbols of divine presence in creation.[27]

These images also had significant meanings for the people in pre-Columbian El Salvador, not too dissimilar from Fernando's interpretation. For the Mayans, deer represented strength, protection, and the four levels of existence: physical, mental, emotional and spiritual. Corn was more than a crop. Its four colors symbolize the creation of human beings: white corn for bone; yellow corn, muscle; black corn, eyes and hair; and red corn, blood. A tree is the tree of life, birth, growth, reproduction, and passing into darkness, the other world. It is a symbol of love and family, the fruit representing offspring. The turkey symbolizes love and the celebration of marriage. These vivid images captured the imagination of the village artists and their customers. Perhaps not everyone attached a spiritual meaning to the images as Fernando did, but Salvadorans everywhere could identify with them.

Fernando worked with a variety of media, including wood, metal, canvas, paper and clay. He referred to the technique he used as the "temple technique" and described it this way:

> When beginning a work, I first divide the painting into individual sections, a step that is very similar to how mosaic artists approach their work. I work on top of malleable surfaces, scraping it and making incisions in it for the lines of the work in progress. The final painting is a process of layering and glazing.[28]

Sinfonía de Colores (fig. 18) illustrates this technique in a stunning departure from the pastoral collage in figure 17 above. Fernando cut and layered the paint much like a stained-glass window.

The strong, angular lines suggest energy and excitement. Eyes are prominent among the scattered leaves. The mandala, a series of rings which represents the universe, is so tiny it is barely visible. Fernando disguises a multitude of birds among abstract shapes, leaves and houses, and layers of vivid colors.

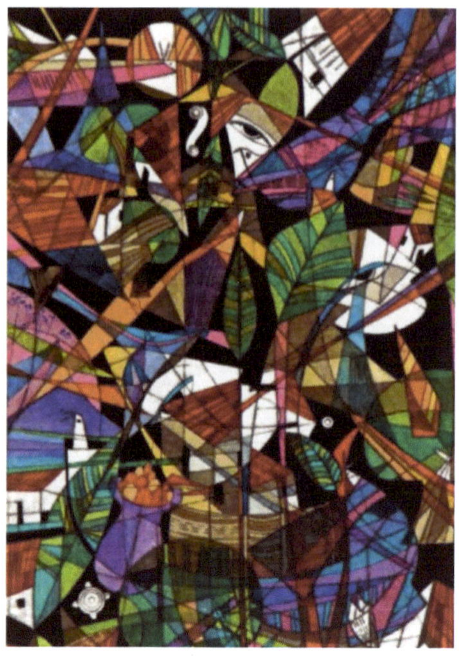

18. *Sinfonía de Colores* (Symphony of Colors),
Fernando Llort, 1988.
Fernando Llort Foundation.

A mixed-media collage depicting the life and environment of La Palma offers another glimpse of Fernando's imagination, his unique birds, and symbolic depiction of a village community (fig. 19). The composition teases the viewer to discover secrets and marvel at its details. Observers who look carefully among the images will find eight humans, a mandala, an angel, a deer, a horse, an armadillo, and six birds, including a parrot and a turkey. Small houses, a winding road and trees, leaves and flowers fill the countryside below the mountains.

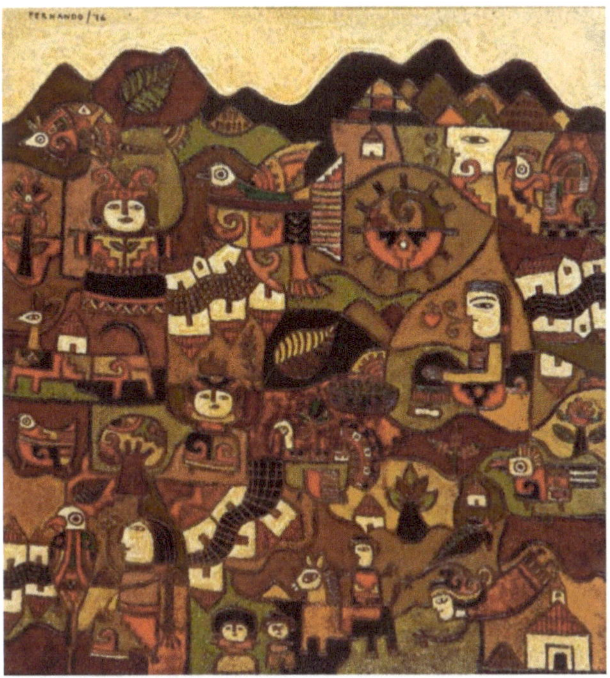

19. *País de La Palma* (Countryside of La Palma),
Fernando Llort, 1976. Fernando Llort Foundation.

On the surface, most of his paintings are his interpretation of the contemporary, rural life of his country. But he often intertwined deliberate echoes of pre-Columbian El Salvador. The people in figure 19 wear clothing and headdresses that recall the Mayans, and the bold, simplified lines of the sun and animal images harken back to ancient imagery.

Fernando believed that the destruction of its ancient culture left El Salvador weakened, even impoverished. He sensed that Salvadorans would never feel whole until that connection to the past was somehow restored. Research has shown that Fernando was right about that. A country's identity is closely connected to the icons and symbols of its past. Without this connection, the country has no roots.[29] Its citizens lack an identity. Fernando intended to restore this connection. Restore the people's cultural roots.

Fernando's Amazing Birds

When he wasn't teaching art classes, Fernando tried different styles and compositions to portray the rural countryside and people of El Salvador. Birds are a constant presence in his paintings, as they are in El Salvador. Sometimes they are the focus. More often they are elements in a scene, abstract or disguised (fig. 20).

Some of Fernando's birds recall those created by pre-Columbian artists who carved them in stone or molded them out of clay. The Mayan bird whistle in figure 21 has a rounded shape, a large beak and prominent eyes, and its head is adorned with feathers circling it like a collar and head-dress. Its feet even have toes or claws, and there is a suggestion of power or arrogance in its de-meanor, perhaps indicating that it is a bird deity. There are remnants of gold and blue pigment, in-dicating that it may have been brightly painted.

Fernando's ceramic bird whistle is more mod-est and even friendly looking (fig. 22). However, it shares the shape, the prominent beak and large eyes, and even the stylized head feathers of its Mayan "ancestor."

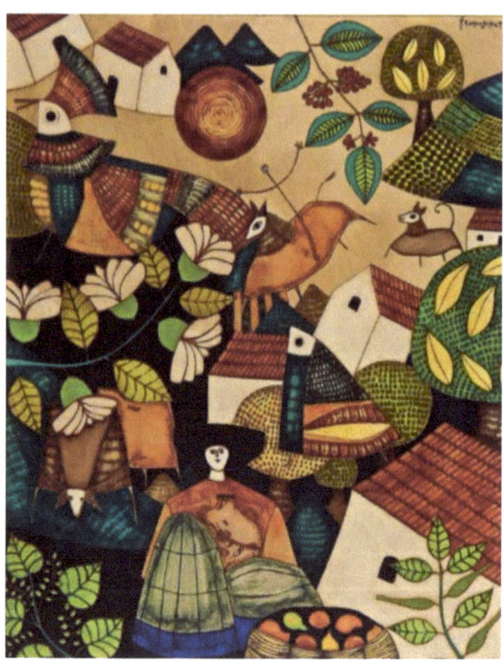

20. *Vida y Color* (Life and Color),
Fernando Llort, 1980.
Fernando Llort Foundation.

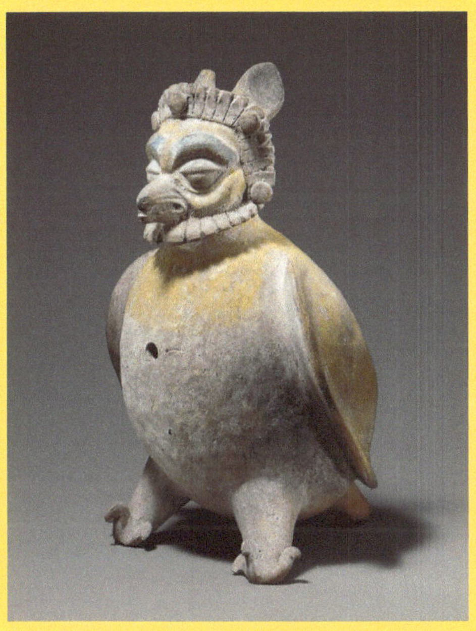

21. Mayan bird whistle, 7th-9th Century, Metropolitan Museum of Art, New York, NY. Free use photo.

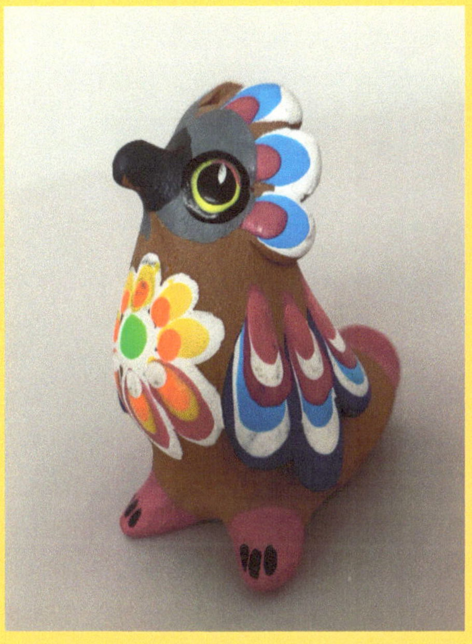

22. Ceramic bird whistle from the studio of Fernando Llort, 2015. Private collection.

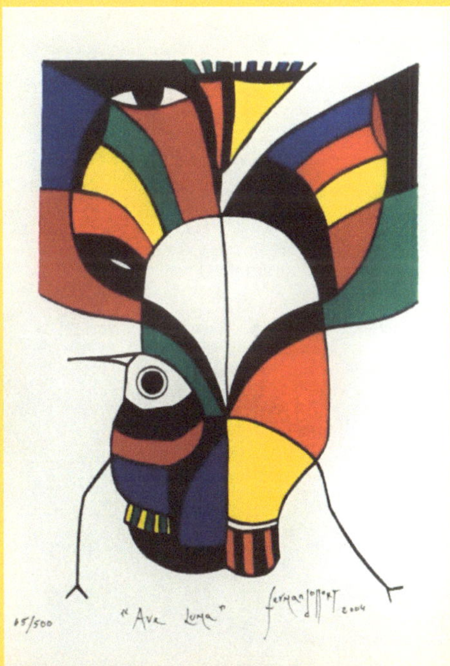

23. *Ave Luna* (Moon Bird), Fernando Llort, 2004. Llort family photo collection.

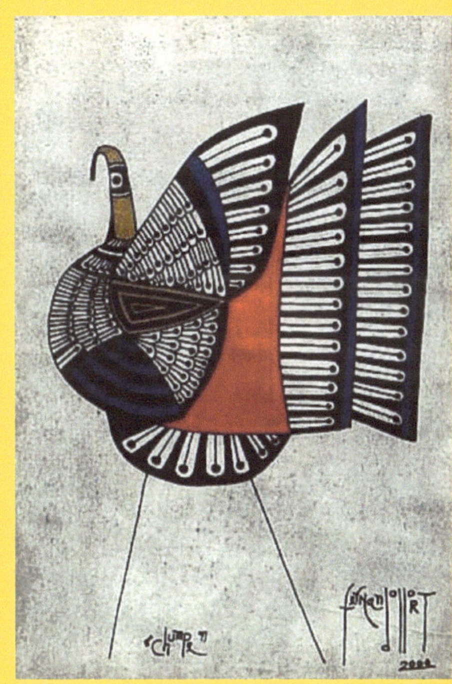

24. *Chumpe* (Turkey), Fernando Llort, 2000. Fernando Llort Foundation.

Ave Luna and *Chumpe* are a striking contrast with each other as well as with Fernando's other birds. With its distinct pattern of bright colors, separated by dark lines and white space, *Ave Luna* seems cheerful and free-spirited. In contrast, *Chumpe* is almost entirely black and gray, set off with a single red accent. Its feathers are delineated with fine detail, and it has a structured, almost architectural look. Although both are whimsical and abstracted, the two images appear opposites in style.

Strong Women

Fernando had tremendous respect for women and objected to their treatment as inferior human beings. He intentionally portrayed female figures as independent and strong. When asked whether he saw himself as a human rights activist, Fernando replied, "Yes, because at that time [when he started the workshops] women's roles were limited to being a housekeeper. The workshops allowed women to work and increased their dignity. Some women learned to drive and came into San Salvador to sell their wares. Some husbands and wives worked together side by side in the workshops."[30]

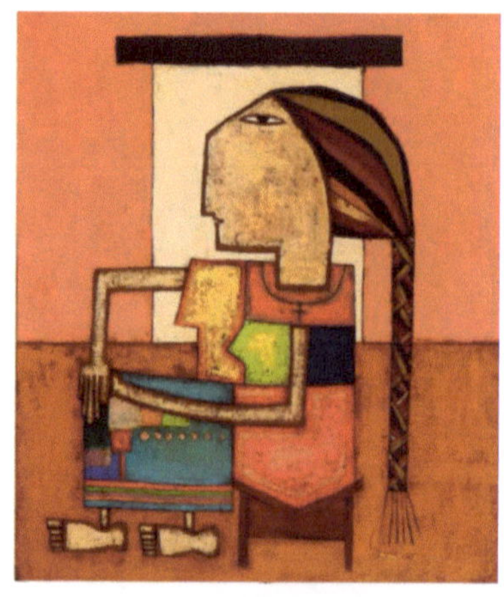

25. *Mujer Sentada* (Seated Woman), Fernando Llort, 1976. Fernando Llort Foundation.

The figure in *Mujer Sentada* (fig. 25) may represent indigenous women with her almond-shaped eyes and long, braided hair. Her bare feet and lack of adornment, apart from a modest cross, hint that she is a simple villager. But seen through Fernando's eyes, she has poise and dignity.

The untitled painting in figure 26 depicts a very different woman. She appears in a headdress, perhaps signifying her social rank, and she is holding or lifting a colorful turkey. The work has no title, so the observer is left to wonder who and what the artist intended to represent—an indigenous ancestor? A priestess? Is she reclining like Mayan royalty or standing in front of a ceremonial table? Offering the turkey or receiving

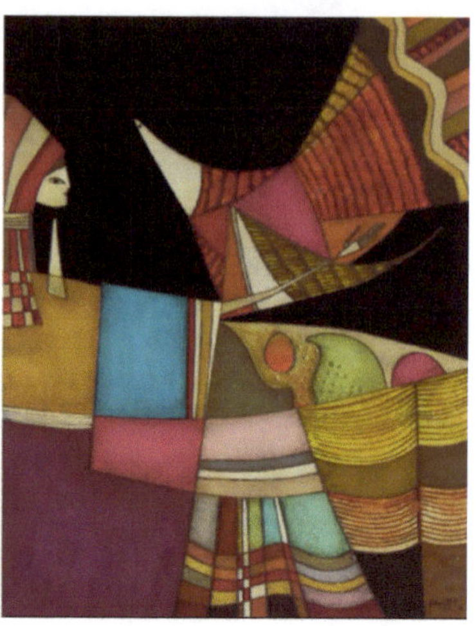

26. Untitled, Fernando Llort. Fernando Llort Foundation.

it? Is she speaking to the turkey? Whatever Fernando intended, the composition is intriguing and pleasing to the eye. And whoever she is, the woman in the portrait communicates dignity and power.

The Sun

Whatever his trouble or loss, Fernando held on to hope and the ideals that always inspired his work. It is possible that the sun, an ever-present symbol of the Creator in his paintings, also represented hope. Fernando painted the sun overlooking the mountains, the villages, and people, in his vision of the sun and earth and all its creatures living in harmony (figs. 27, 28).

The sun motif extended to his music as well. It is in the name of his band, *La Banda del Sol*, and in the lyrics of *Abriendo Camino* (Opening the Way), one of their most popular recordings.

Fernando and the others sang *"Abriendo camino voy, viendo la luz del sol brillar..."* (I am opening the way, watching the light of the brilliant sun).[31]

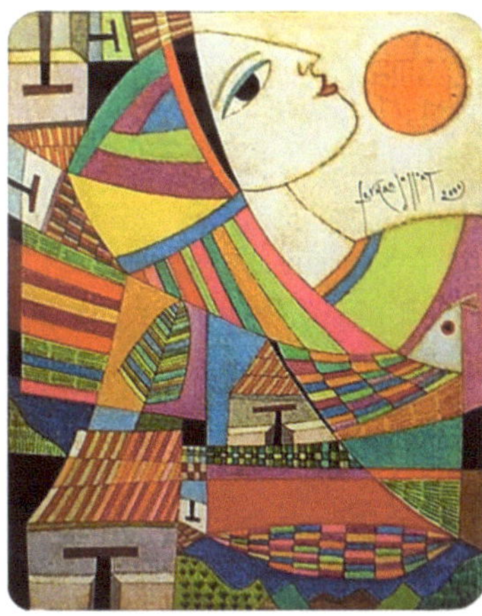

27. *El Beso del Sol* (The Kiss of the Sun), Fernando Llort, 2000. Fernando Llort Foundation.

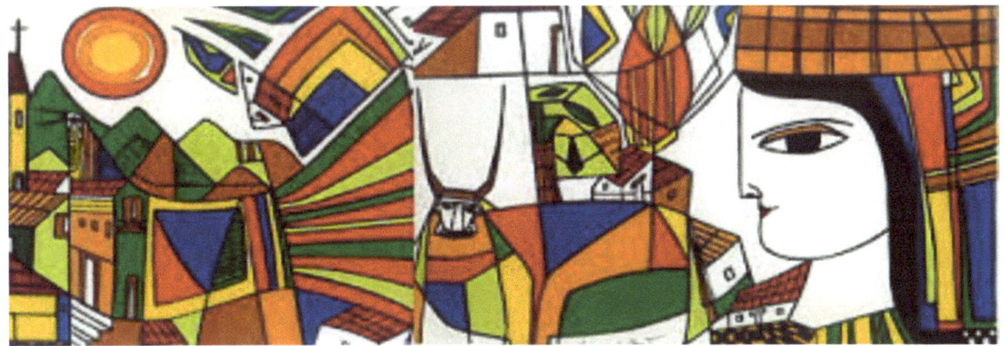

28. *Llena Mi Canasto* (Fill My Basket), Fernando Llort, 2018. Fernando Llort Foundation.

Inspired by Nature

Fernando always found inspiration in the woods and mountains, and he wanted to share the experience with the young artists. He taught them to pay close attention to their surroundings so they wouldn't miss seeing the wild orchid, or the deer or parrot among the trees (figs. 29, 30). Day after day, he helped them discover the joy of creation, the joy of art, and the joy of working with their hands.

When Fernando and his family moved to San Salvador a few years later, local artist José Anibal Fuentes spoke of similar experiences when Fernando took him and others on excursions to La Palma.[32]

One of the earliest students in La Palma, Roberto Burgos, said that Fernando's faith and his love of nature helped the students to observe and appreciate more deeply the beauty of their surroundings. They came to believe, as Fernando did, that making art was a special calling, a way to praise creation.[33]

> *"They were very talented,"* Fernando said of the villagers. *"I just turned them on."*[34]

Roberto described what happened in La Palma this way: "Fernando would awaken the art that was asleep inside them."[35]

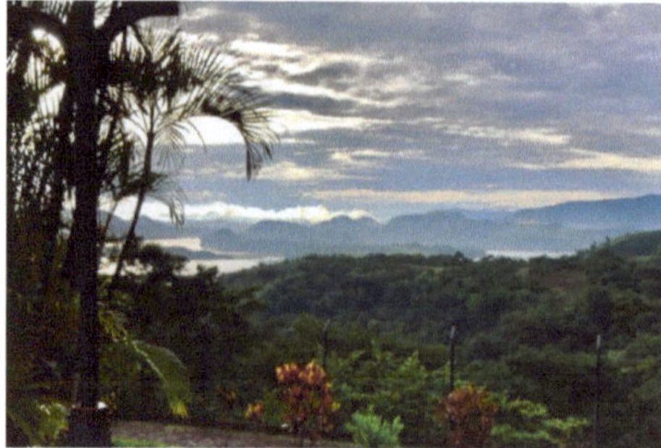

29. Sunrise over the mountains of El Salvador, 2021. Author's photo.

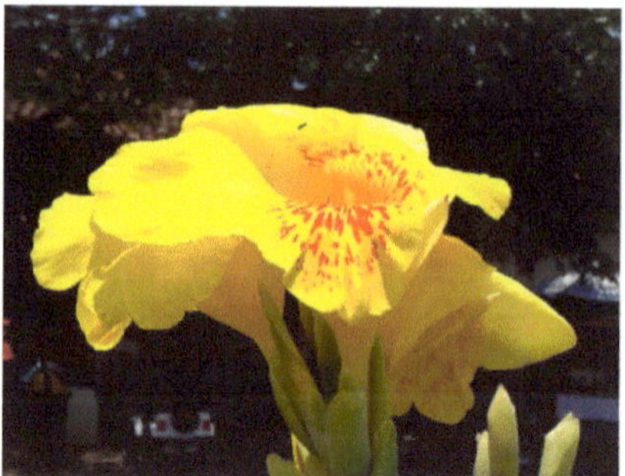

30. *Lycaste Lasioglossa* Orchid, 2021. Author's photo.

Life in La Palma

As time passed, La Palma became known as an artisan village. Fernando encouraged the artists to add variety to their crafts, so they made small wooden boxes, wall hangings, and ceramics decorated with his designs. They also embroidered blouses, and painted wooden Nativity sets. To sell their work, they took buses up and down the mountain into San Salvador and to other villages. Their handcrafts were inexpensive and popular, and customers often came to them. As their income increased, the artists and their families were able to save money for the first time.

> *"Many people live off of the work that is done in La Palma," Fernando said, "and this gives me great joy and satisfaction."*[36]

However, Fernando did not want to be the leader of a factory of workers who were dependent on him. Instead, he wanted the artists and crafters to get together to share equally in the work and benefits of their growing enterprise. So in 1977, he and helped the artists organize a cooperative, *La Semilla de Dios* (The Seed of God), named for the copinol seed. Members of the cooperative would produce and market their crafts together and share the costs of materials and the profits equally (fig. 31).

Hearing about the La Palma workshops and remembering Fernando's work at the *Forma* in San Salvador, master artist Carlos Cañas came to La Palma in 1978. While the village artists already carved designs in wood, his classes in etching enabled them to apply their designs to tile, slate, and glass.

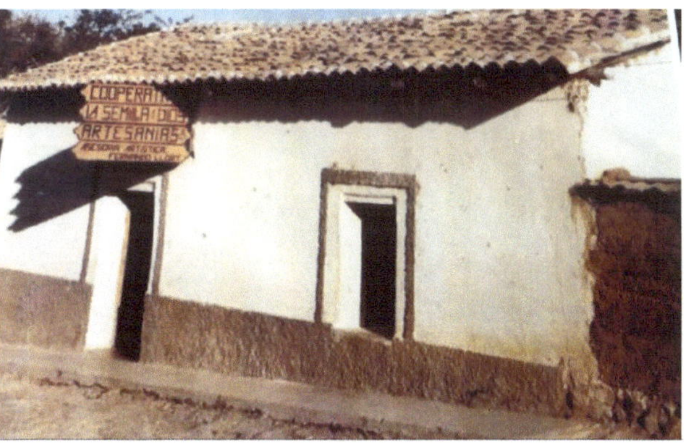

31. Original location of *La Semilla de Dios* cooperative, 1977.
Llort family photo collection.

The workshops multiplied, but Fernando's friends were gradually drawn in other directions. His best friend Tamba, a poet and musician with whom he had written songs, felt called to fight the government's oppression. He joined the rebels and was later killed in battle. Fernando grieved for his friend. He grieved for everyone who suffered because of the war, the innocent villagers as well as the fighters. He shared Tamba's desire for justice and equality, but his way to spread peace was through art. His joyful paintings, the simplicity of his life, and his dedication to the people of La Palma all testified to his faith in a God of love and justice and peace. Not killing. Not war.

Fernando stayed in La Palma, committed to his family, his painting, and the growing community of artisans (fig. 32). He counseled them, encouraged them, and inspired them. Over time, the artists began to look upon Fernando as their father, and even their spiritual leader.

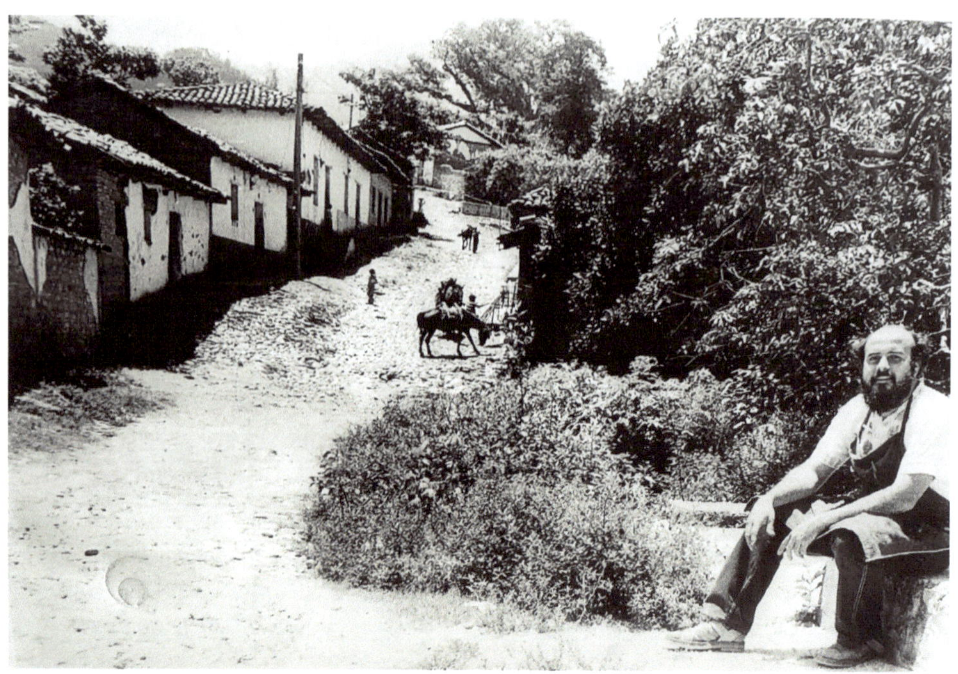

32. Fernando in La Palma, 1980s. Llort family photo collection.

Of course, there were always people with troubles, and Fernando gave his help without hesitation. His son Juan Pablo remembered one day on the way to school when they drove past a poor, desperate-looking man on the road. Fernando continued on so they wouldn't be late, but Juan Pablo found out later that Fernando had gone back to pick up the man, brought him home, invited him to wash, and gave him clean clothes. Then his father sat with the man as his mother prepared a meal for him.

> *"He taught us compassion,"* Juan Pablo said, *"and I have always tried to follow his example."*[37]

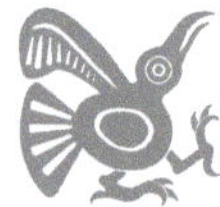

A LONG WAR

While art was thriving in La Palma in the 1970s, misery and exploitation persisted in the country, and protests grew bigger. The militia was charged to keep order, and they began to increase their use of intimidation and violence. Between 1979 and 1981, death squads in El Salvador murdered 30,000 people.[38] The beloved Archbishop Óscar Romero was assassinated in March 1980, and thousands came for his funeral, overflowing the Cathedral. Snipers fired on the mourners from nearby rooftops, killing and wounding over 200 people. Soon afterward, the whole country exploded into a vicious civil war.

To avoid capture, the rebels, members of the *Farabundo Martí* National Liberation Front, moved to mountain encampments and caves. Their families were threatened with retaliation, and so they moved to the mountains too, tending the wounded, teaching the children, and trying to avoid detection as military helicopters searched overhead. Authorized to crush dissension or signs of guerrilla sympathy, government soldiers massacred civilians, at times entire villages. Guerrilla troops responded with assassinations and atrocities of their own. For 12 years, the violence went on, killing both the innocent and the combatants.

Fernando had spent years nurturing art and a sense of community among the people of La Palma, and the villagers wanted to make art, not war. When soldiers marched into La Palma looking for rebels, they found artists at work. Instead of threatening the villagers, the soldiers held out their rifles and asked the artists to paint their names and insignias on them.[39] When the government troops were gone, rebel guerrillas also appeared in La Palma, and they too wanted their names and insignias painted on their rifle butts.

Guerilla leaders knew how much the villagers looked up to Fernando, so they asked him if they could speak to the people about their cause. Fernando refused to jeopardize the lives in his beloved community. He said no, that La Palma was not at war and the artists were too busy at their work. Fernando's courage gave confidence and hope to the people.

But the village was not spared from the violence. At times, families had to huddle on the floor in their homes while soldiers shouted outside and bullets shattered their windows. Fernando's children recalled the night that their grandfather, Estela's father, was mistaken for a combatant and shot. Unable to get help because of the shooting in the street, his grieving family could only comfort him while he died.[40]

Fernando and his family were looking forward to moving in to their new home in La Palma when they received anonymous death threats. In the middle of a civil war, he didn't know which side had targeted him, or whether the threats were politically motivated. It could have been the guerrillas, angry at his refusal to let them recruit in the village. Or it could have been government forces, suspicious that he was supporting the rebels. Either way, to stay would jeopardize the village as well as his family. He had no choice but to leave his beloved La Palma. The family stayed with friends in Mexico until the culprits were caught. Then they returned to the country and settled in San Salvador.

Starting Again

Fernando built another studio in his garage where he resumed his painting and started new workshops (fig. 33). He named his new studio *El Arbol de Dios* (The Tree of God), and with Estela's help he expanded his artisan movement, once again teaching his style and techniques and helping the artists market their products. He exhibited his paintings and created new color palettes and experimented with glass. His compositions never veered from portraying the joyous symbols of village life, as if in defiance of the fear, the killing, and destruction of the war.

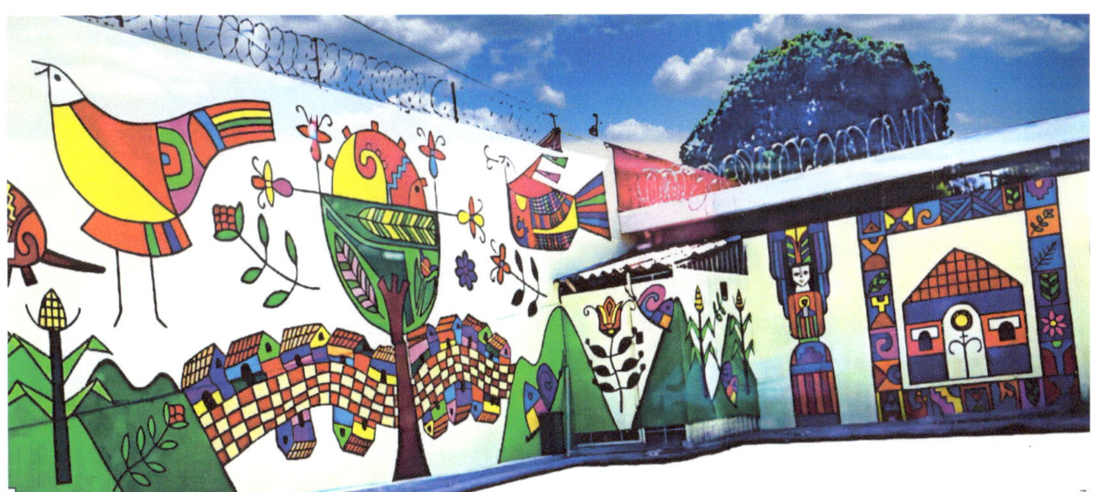

33. Painted wall at the front of *El Arbol de Dios* in San Salvador, current location of shop and art studio. Llort family photo collection.

To Fernando, creating art sparks an awakening inside a person. An awakening to the beauty of patterns, colors, and textures in the world, especially in nature. He also believed that creating art is a powerful healer, ultimately stirring up renewed hope and confidence in oneself. Seeing the transformation of La Palma, Fernando was determined to assure creative opportunities for young people. They should know what it is to be inspired, to feel the joy of working with their hands and creating beauty. To be transformed like the clay.

He and Estela set up the Fernando Llort Foundation in 1989 to secure art education in El Salvador, hoping to inspire young people to choose careers in art and to grow as individuals. Since then, the Foundation has become a valuable resource for young people. Its programs are especially helpful to discourage gang influence and to support those who are looking for ways to overcome poverty and lack of education. The classes introduce them to art experiences such as painting, sewing, and carpentry, and help them to develop leadership and marketing skills.

And Then Peace

In 1984, leaders of the rebel *Farabundo Martí* National Liberation Front met with President José Napoleón Duarte and other government and military officials in La Palma to negotiate an end to the war, but they were unsuccessful. Finally, in 1992, the guerrilla leaders and Duarte's successor, President Alfredo Cristiani, signed the Chapultepec Peace Accords in Mexico City. At last, the war was over. By the time the fighting ended, over 75,000 people had been killed—men, women, and children—and countless others had disappeared.[41]

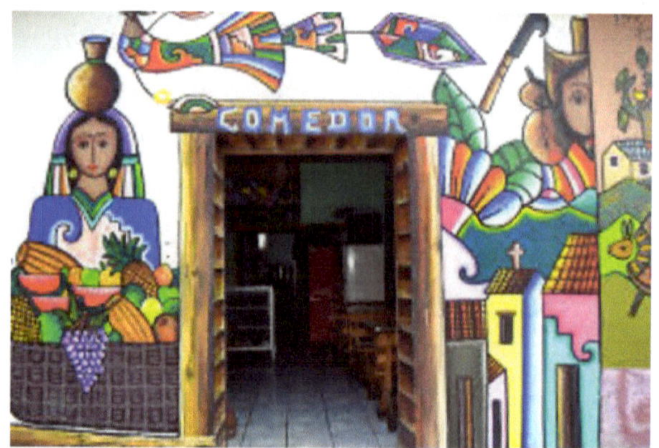

34. Store entrance in La Palma with images painted by local artisans. Llort family photo collection.

El Salvador mourned for the dead and rejoiced that the war was over. The villagers of La Palma celebrated with paint. After they repaired their homes and shops, residents and shopkeepers asked the artists to decorate their buildings with the images Fernando taught them. Today, decades later, colorful birds, flowers, *casitas*, and other symbols of their everyday life still appear on doors, walls and even street posts along the roads in many villages beyond La Palma (fig. 34).

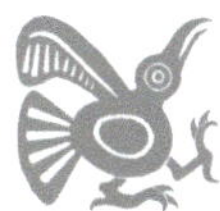

AN EXTRAORDINARY ASSIGNMENT: THE CATHEDRAL MURAL

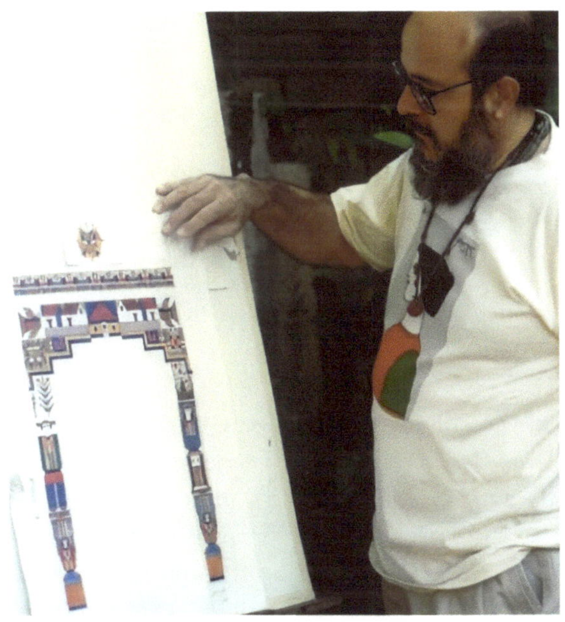

35. Fernando with his design for the mural, 1999. Llort family photo collection.

THE ART OF LA PALMA HAD SURVIVED THE WAR, but all over El Salvador, people needed healing, and damages needed repair, including the Cathedral of San Salvador. For forty-three years, the building had suffered from earthquakes, neglect, and then damage from the war. In 1997, when repairs began, Fernando Llort's art was known around the world and praised by the Ministry of Foreign Commerce and Salvadoran Chamber of Tourism.[42]

Familiar with his artistic style, the architect overseeing the restoration of the Cathedral recommended Fernando to design the entrance. As a result, the *Fundación Catedral* and Archbishop Fernando Sáenz Lacalle commissioned him to create and install a mural around the Cathedral's front door to celebrate the peace. All of San Salvador looked forward to the restoration of the Cathedral and its decoration by their beloved artist.

Fernando spent a year planning his design—an arc of tiles portraying symbols of the faith and cultural heritage of El Salvador (fig. 35). Each tile was carefully measured at 25x25 centimeters (approximately one foot by one foot). It would reach twenty-two meters (72 feet) high and required 2,700 tiles to cover its surface.[43]

He asked his three children, artist José Anibal Fuentes, and Anibal's two sisters to assist him. Together they cut, painted, glazed and numbered each tile by hand. After the tiles were fired, they were carefully laid out, one at a time, on the open floor of the Cathedral (fig. 36).

Then Fernando directed eight workers as they transferred the tiles and affixed them to their correct positions around the Cathedral entrance. Three weeks later, he gazed at the most significant work of his life: a portrayal of the people of El Salvador, reflecting not the rich upper class, but the *campesinos* (farmers), the working class, and indigenous people.

Hearing the work was done, onlookers gathered in the morning at Plaza Barrios. They stared upward as shadows disappeared, and the sun brightened the indigo sky. Then they gasped with amazement and joy, seeing symbols of themselves, their villages, their faith, and even their crops, decorating the entrance of their historic cathedral.

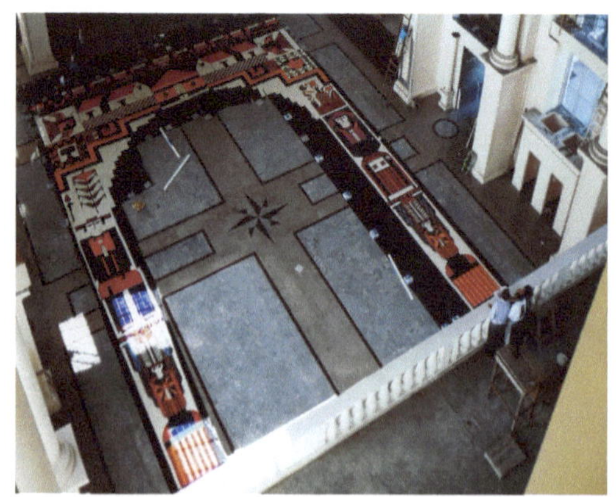

36. Assembled tiles on the floor inside the San Salvador Cathedral, 1999. Llort family photo collection.

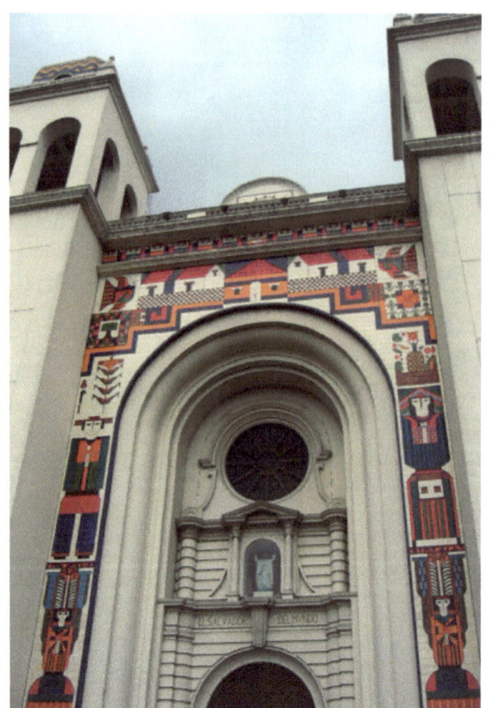

37. Cathedral mural, Fernando Llort, inaugurated in 1999. Free use photo.

All of these images—the houses, trees, the ears of corn, birds, farmers, and geometric symbols—were religious symbols in Fernando's mind. They represented Creator God, always present in the world, especially in nature, much like the spiritual beliefs of pre-Columbian peoples. Its title, *La Armonía de mi Pueblo*, The Harmony of My People, expressed Fernando's gratitude for peace and harmony in his homeland and his hope for harmony among all creation (figs. 37, 38).

In March 1999, thousands gathered in Plaza Barrios to inaugurate the restored San Salvador Cathedral and to recognize the colorful folk images of their local artist Fernando Llort.

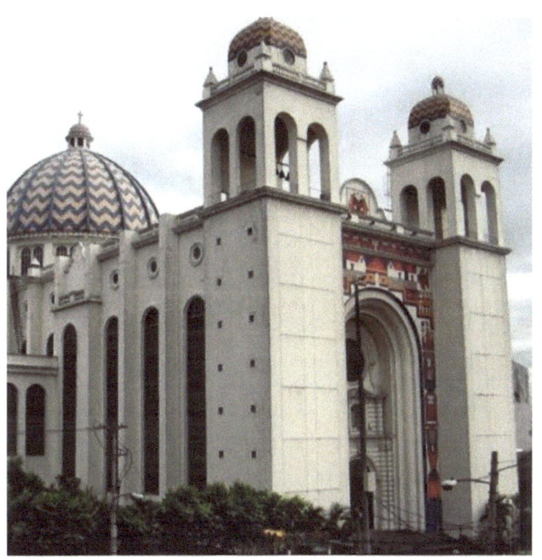

38. 1998 restoration of the Metropolitan Cathedral of San Salvador with the Fernando Llort mural. Free use photo.

"The mural represented a way of remembering the civil war years and giving them closure," artist Óscar Jiménez of La Palma explained. "It spoke about mankind, work, family, faith and everything that constitutes harmony."[44]

Fernando's masterpiece, the Cathedral mural, drew even more attention to his art and more invitations to exhibit all over the world. While Fernando continued to experiment with his own art, he also taught art to students in San Salvador and visited the artists in La Palma. But he wanted to share his message about the power of art. He said yes to the invitations and brought his paintings to communities around the United States, Europe, Japan, Canada and South America.

The Outrage

One night in late December of 2011, a team of workers came to Plaza Barrios in San Salvador. First, they constructed scaffolding. Then they hung a huge curtain between the bell towers to hide the front of the Cathedral. Finally, with their chisels and jackhammers, they climbed up the scaffolding (fig. 39).

During the hours that followed, their pounding echoed over the entire city as they broke and dislodged all 2,700 tiles. By the end of the day, Fernando's masterpiece lay shattered on the plaza below.

When Fernando and his family heard about the mural's demolition, they were astounded. No one had suggested that his mural was threatened. The Llort family and friends hurried to the Cathedral and retrieved pieces of the broken tiles (fig. 40), but they were sent away. Instead, heavy equipment was brought in to remove the broken pieces.

"It was the saddest day of my life," Fernando said.[45]

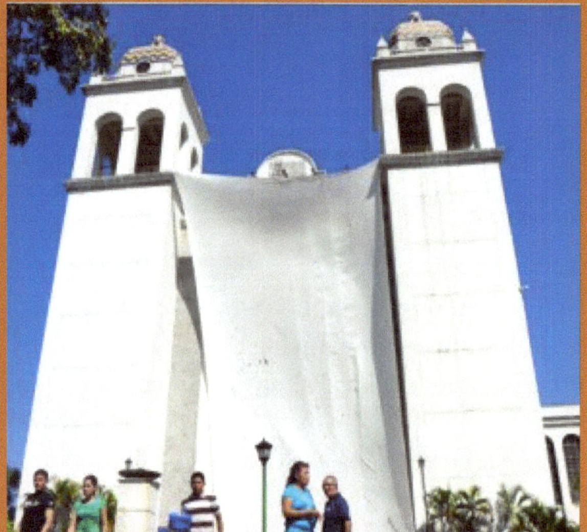

39. Cathedral mural hidden from view, 2011.
From the collection of *Indignados por el Mural.*

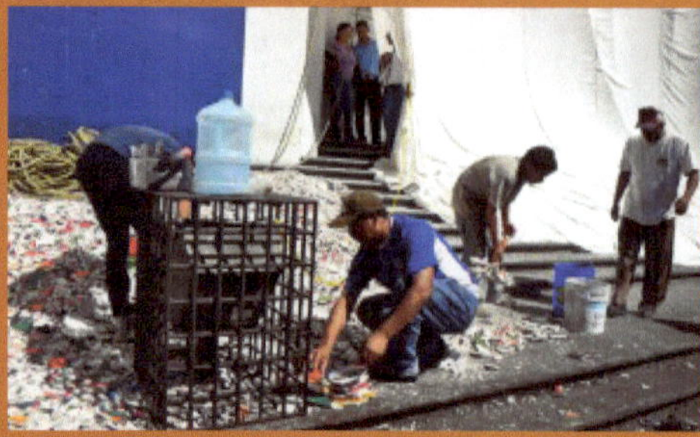

40. Llort family and friends collecting
broken tiles from the mural, 2012.
From the collection of *Indignados por el Mural.*

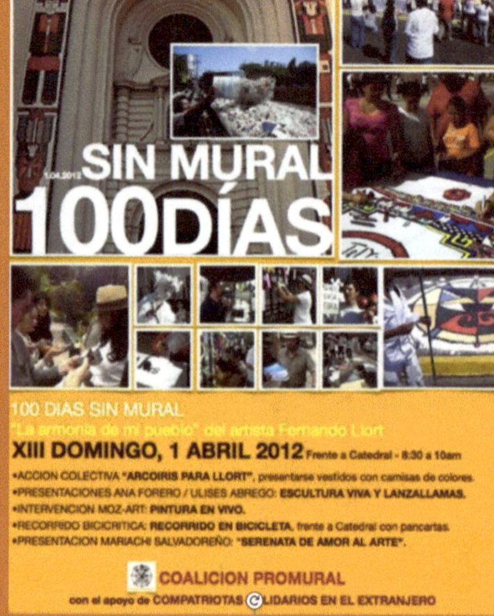

42. "100 Days Without the Mural" Poster
announcing a demonstration to protest the
destruction of Fernando's mural, 2012.
Indignados por el Mural.

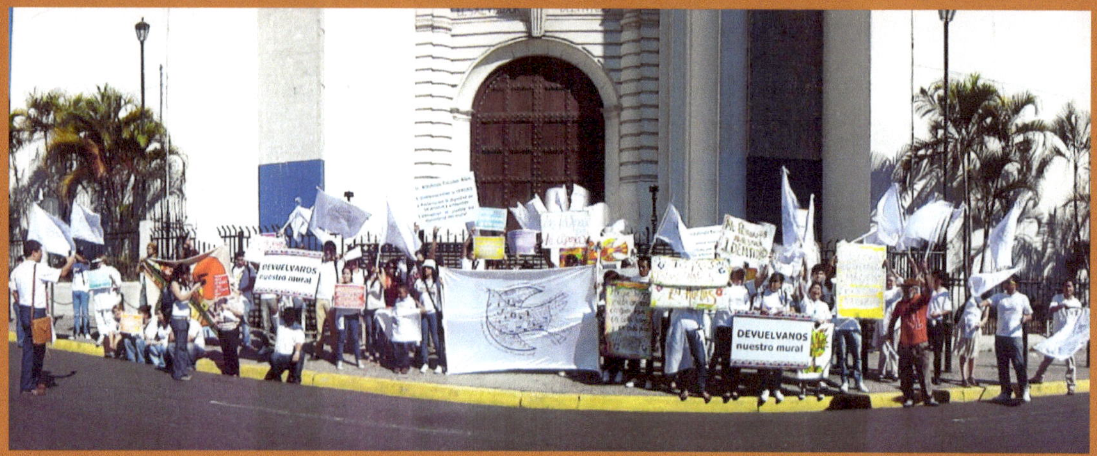

41. Demonstrators in front of the Cathedral, its mural gone, 2012.
Photo from the collection of *Indignados por el Mural.*

City officials were as outraged as the public that this city icon had been destroyed. The Secretary of Culture of El Salvador condemned the action. Eventually, the Archbishop of San Salvador, José Luis Escobar Alas, acknowledged that he had ordered removal of the mural.

Fernando and his family were told that the tiles were cracked and falling, a danger to visitors; that the colors were fading; that the mural featured secular symbols rather than religious ones. But there was no evidence of physical deterioration, and during twelve years no concerns had been expressed about its symbols.[46]

When asked about these reasons for the mural's destruction, Fernando said, "I don't believe the explanation that was given. I was confused because I always thought I created this work for God; that everything in it had religious symbolism. So I didn't understand why an authority of the church would not like religious symbolism."[47]

In a press conference he and his family held after the mural's destruction, he spoke for artists everywhere with these words: "I have always believed that our hands were made to construct, not to destroy." He added, "I feel surprised and immeasurably saddened because they [the Church] have refused to give me the opportunity to reclaim with dignity the most important work of my life."[48]

No explanation could soothe the anger and grief felt by the thousands of Salvadorans and international visitors who had been inspired by the mural. Artisans came from the city and countryside to protest its destruction.

Some painted reproductions of the mural on large pieces of cloth and held them in demonstrations (figs. 41, 42). Others waved signs that said, "We are your true mural and no one can tear us down."[49] Although the protests continued for weeks, and objections from state and city officials and cultural agencies mounted, diocesan representatives offered little defense of their action.

Overlooking Plaza Barrios now is a plain, undecorated stucco facade.

The Mural of Broken Pieces

In spite of his pain over the mural's destruction, Fernando persevered. He had accepted the invitation to design the Cathedral façade with the same faith that inspired his life. With each tile and each stroke of paint, Fernando had celebrated reconciliation and the beauty of the country he loved.

Fernando responded to the destruction of his mural in the same way he lived. Instead of giving in to anger, he transformed violence and brokenness into a message of peace and love and welcome. As he put it, "At that moment it caused me sadness, it was hard for me, but I turned that page to live a positive present in which that no longer counts. And I think that mural lives in everyone's heart."[50]

> *"He always told me, you have to do all things with love,"* said his daughter María José. *"If you do it like this, everything will be fine."*[51]

The Llort family were able to collect enough of the broken tiles for Fernando to design and create another, different mural only months later. Named "Fraternal Hug," the set of murals and sculptures welcomes visitors and returning Salvadorans just outside the airport, south of San Salvador (figs. 43, 44).

And so Fernando's mural still exists. It still proclaims love and joy. Its very existence proclaims that separation and brokenness can be healed.

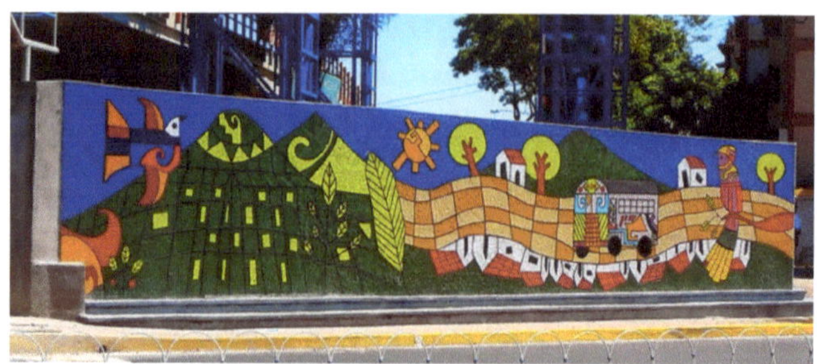

43. Mosaic section of *Abrazo Fraterno* (Fraternal Hug) Mural, composed of broken tiles from the Cathedral, 2012. Llort family photo collection.

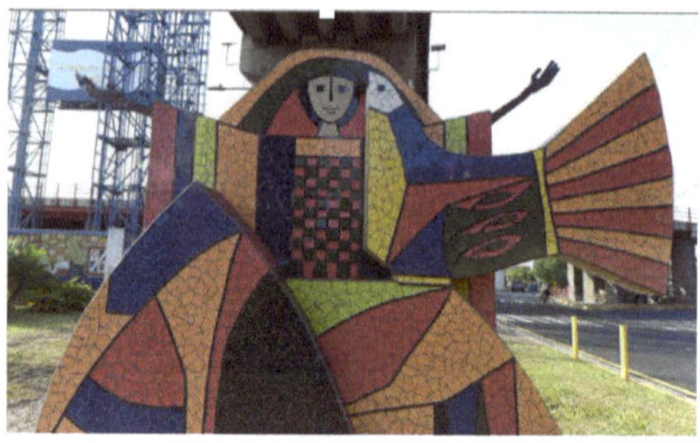

44. *Abrazo Fraterno* (Fraternal Hug) sculpture, part of the mural composed of broken Cathedral tiles, 2012. Llort family photo collection.

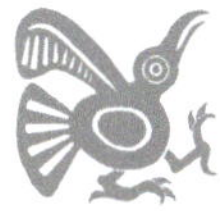

THE LEGACY OF FERNANDO LLORT

THE LOSS OF HIS MASTERPIECE WAS AN UNSPEAKABLE TRAGEDY, but Fernando's greatest legacy is a *living* mural—a living Harmony of My People. It is the story that began fifty years earlier when Fernando boarded the bus to that little mountain village of La Palma. It is the story of the lives transformed because Fernando Llort shared his vision and imagination with the people of La Palma. And it is the story of a country whose people found pride in their ancestry because of this same vision.

Fernando continued to paint, experiment with glass and other media, and to exhibit his work around the world. In 2013, he was asked to design and paint the Romero Cross in memory of martyred Archbishop Óscar Romero. This twelve-foot cross stands in St. George's Cathedral in Southwark, London, England.

His family expanded the programs of the Fernando Llort Foundation. Since its beginning in 1989, more than 4,000 children, young people and adults have participated in these leadership programs and art projects.

Fernando's greatest legacy lies with the artisans and their cooperatives in La Palma who transformed from a village of subsistence farming into a community of self-supporting artisans and a major tourist destination. Fifty years since those first classes in La Palma, the villagers' crafts are sold all over the world, and Fernando's artistic style has become a symbol of the culture and folk art of El Salvador. Over 10,000 people have earned a living through art since that first workshop in 1972.

Fernando continued to share his talent and his stories until his death on August 10, 2018, when he was 69 years old.

In his tribute to Fernando Llort, Salvadoran President Salvador Sánchez Cerén stated, "His charisma, masterful works and affection for our people capture the cultural identity and the development in peace and harmony of our nation."[52]

Fernando showed that art can reawaken the soul of an entire country. He helped a village build its future, and he helped the people of his country reclaim their past.

NOTES

1   Hernández, Evelia. "Mi padre siempre compraba una camioneta…" El Diario De Hoy, November 8, 2016.

2   Interview with Fernando Llort.

3   According to the Oxford Dictionary, the term plastic arts is used to describe "art forms that involve modeling or molding, such as sculpture and ceramics, or art involving the representation of solid objects with three-dimensional effects."

4   González, Óscar. *"Falleció el ceramista salvadoreño y escultor César Sermeño."* *La Prensa Gráfica,* May 8, 2018.

5   Doyle, James. "Ancient Maya Sculpture." *Heilbrunn Timeline of Art History.* New York: The Metropolitan Museum of Art, 2000.

6   Interview with Fernando Llort.

7   *Ibid.*

8   *Ibid.*

9   Smith, Victoria C., Antonio Costa, and Gerardo Aguirre-Díaz et al. "The Magnitude and Impact of the 431 CE *Tierra Blanca Joven* Eruption of Ilopango, El Salvador." *Proceedings of the National Academy of Sciences of the United States of America (PNAS),* v. 117, No. 42.

10 Alexander Koch, Chris Brierley, Mark Maslin, and Simon Lewis. "European colonisation of the Americas killed 10% of world population and caused global cooling." *The Conversation,* University College London, January 31, 2019. https://theconversation.com/us/topics/central-america-11994?page=2. (Estimating death toll in the Americas caused by colonization of "56m by the beginning of the 1600s – 90% of the pre-Columbian indigenous population and around 10% of the global population at the time.")

11 Fernando Llort website. https://www.fernando-llort.com.

12 Interview with Fernando Llort.

13 *Ibid.*

14 Caute, David. *The Year of the Barricades: A Journey Through 1968.* NY: Harper and Row, 1988.

15 Chavez, Joaquin M. *"Operación amor,* hippies, musicians… in El Salvador." *The Routledge Handbook of the Global Sixties: Between Protest and Nation-Building.* Chen Jiam, Martin Klimke, Masha Kirasirova, Mary Nolan, *et al.* London: Routledge, 2018.

[16] *Ibid.*

[17] Huezo Mixco, Miguel. "Julia Díaz, patron saint of Salvadoran painting." http://archive.laprensa.com.sv/1991107/revista_dominical/rd01.asp.

[18] Interview with Fernando Llort.

[19] Molina, Rodolfo Francisco, curator. *Exhibición Retrospectiva de Fernando Llort, Sala Nacional de Exposiciónes Salarrué,* 2012.

[20] Fernando Llort website.

[21] *Ibid.*

[22] María José Llort Instagram post, October 26, 2020.

[23] Fernando Llort website.

[24] *Ibid.*

[25] Huezo Mixco, Miguel. "El Salvador and the Construction of Cultural Identity." *Inter-American Development Bank*, October, 1999—No. 34, pp. 8-9.

[26] Molina, Rodolfo Francisco, curator. *Exhibición Retrospectiva de Fernando Llort, Sala Nacional de Exposiciónes Salarrué,* 2012.

[27] Interview with Roberto Enrique Burgos.

[28] Fernando Llort website.

[29] Estrada Quiroz, Aldo. "Art and Crafts of La Palma: Color for a New Salvadoran Identity." Fragment of research for a Master's thesis entitled "Arts and Crafts of La Palma: Origins and Trajectory of a Contemporary Cultural Expression of El Salvador." National Autonomous University of Mexico, 2004.

[30] Sheaffer, Caroline J. and Donald J Seiple. Interview with Fernando Llort. *Afflicted with Hope.* January 15, 2014. http://www.embracingelsalvador.org/fernando.llort.

[31] *Abriendo Camino*, composed by Manuel Martínez Daglio, 1971. Translation by María José Llort.

[32] Interview with José Anibal Fuentes.

[33] Interview with Roberto Burgos.

[34] Interview with Fernando Llort.

[35] Interview with Roberto Burgos.

36 Interview with Fernando Llort.

37 Interview with Juan Pablo Llort.

38 Heidenry, Rachel. "El Salvador: The Politics of Art and Memory." *Pulitzer Center on Crisis Reporting*, Washington, DC. February 15, 2012.

39 Interview with Fernando Llort.

40 Interview with Mercedes Llort.

41 Center for Justice and Accountability El Salvador. "Transitional Justice in El Salvador." https://cja.org/what-we-do/transitional-justice-initiatives/el-salvador.

42 Fernando Llort website.

43 *Ibid.*

44 Bermúdez Liévano, Andrés (contributor). "Salvadorans Protest Destruction of Pacifist Mural." Quoting Óscar Jiménez. *The Observer*, March 5, 2012. https://observers.france24.com/en/20120503-salvadorians-protest-destruction-pacifist-mural-el-salvador-cathedral-harmony-of-our-people-tiles-llorta-artist.

45 Interview with Fernando Llort.

46 Heidenry, Rachel. "Archbishop Orders Destruction of Salvadoran Mural." Special to *The Pulitzer Center on Crisis Reporting*, Washington, DC. January 6, 2012.

47 Sheaffer, Caroline J. and Donald J Seiple. Interview with Fernando Llort. *Afflicted with Hope.* January 15, 2014. http://embracingelsalvador.org/fernando.llort.

48 Fernando Llort press conference. https://www.elsalvadorperspectives.com/2012/01/fernando-llort-responds-to-destruction.html.

49 Andrés Bermúdez Liévano, freelance journalist. Posted on the *Indignados por el Mural* Facebook group. May 3, 2012.

50 Menjívar, Élmer L. and María Luz Nóchez. *"Mi dio risa cuando el Arzobispo hablo de un ojo mason."* Interview with Fernando Llort. El Faro Express, November 6, 2013.

51 María José Llort Instagram post, December 30, 2020.

52 Ceren, President Salvador Sanchez, *Alianza* Metropolitan News, August 11, 2018.

BIBLIOGRAPHY

Aragon, Carlos Francisco, "El Planeta de los Cerdos" (The Planet of the Pigs). Lyrics and music by Carlos Francisco Aragon, 1971. From the English transcript for Nicasio Jaragua for the Salvadoran Revolutionary Historical Archive, Index of the MCA, 2010.

Bermúdez Liévano, Andrés, freelance journalist. Posted on the "Indignados por el Mural" Facebook group. May 3, 2012.

Bolivar, Pabel. "Fernando Llort: Mis maestros fueron los Mayas." Diario1.com, December 2, 2013.

Caute, David. The Year of the Barricades: A Journey through 1968. NY: Harper and Row, 1988.

Center for Justice and Accountability El Salvador. "Transitional Justice in El Salvador." https://cja.org/what-we-do/transitional-justice-initiatives/el-salvador.

Chavez, Joaquin M. "Operación amor, hippies, musicians, and cultural transformation in El Salvador." The Routledge Handbook of the Global Sixties: Between Protest and Nation- Building. Chen Jiam, Martin Klimke, Masha Kirasirova, Mary Nolan, et al. London: Routledge, 2018.

Chávez Escobar, Ana Margarita and José Manuel Carranza Bonilla. Las 100 Historias que Siempre Quise Saber: Personas exitosas de El Salvador. San Salvador Editorial G.T.C., 2011.

De La Cruz, Claudia M. "Can art represent a country? In search of Salvadoran Cultural and National Identities through 20th century literature, poetry, and art." Master's thesis. March 29, 2016. https://dukespace.lib.duke.edu/dspace/bitstream/handle/10161/11828/DeLaCruzC-MastersProject-OFICIAL.pdf?sequence=1.

Doyle, James. "Ancient Maya Sculpture." *Heilbrunn Timeline of Art History*. New York: The Metropolitan Museum of Art, 2000.

Estrada Quiroz, Aldo. "Arte y artesanía de La Palma: orígenes y trayectoria de una expresión cultural de El Salvador contemporáñeo." Mexico: August, 2005.

Estrada Quiroz, Aldo. "Artesanías de La Palma: Color for a New Salvadoran Identity." Dec. 2006. Pp. 53-88. Editorial CIDAP Artesanías de America Magazine, No. 62. Project MUSE.

Fernando Llort, "Speech by Fernando Llort as the National Culture Award 2013." El Faro, November 6, 2013.

Fernando Llort website.

Finger, Thomas. "The Art of Fernando Llort." Diálogo: Center for Latino Research, DePaul University. Volume 16, Number 1, Spring 2013, pp. 98-112. Project MUSE, University of Texas Press: 2013.

Gonzalez, Oscar. *"Fallecio el ceramista salvadoreno y escultor Cesar Semeno,"* La Prensa Grafica,
    May 8, 2018. https://www.laprensagrafica.come/cultura/Fallecio-el-ceramista-salvadoreno-
    y-escultor-cesar-Sermeno-20180508-0031.html.

Guevara, Ricardo. "Artesanos en el camino de la superación." El Diario de Hoy, June 20, 2002.

Heidenry, Rachel. "Archbishop Orders Destruction of Salvadoran Mural." Pulitzer Center on
    Crisis Reporting, Washington, DC. January 6, 2012.

Heidenry, Rachel. "El Salvador: The Politics of Art and Memory." Pulitzer Center on Crisis Reporting,
    Washington, DC. February 15, 2012.

Hernández, Evelia. "Mi Padre Siempre Compraba Una Camioneta..." El Diario De Hoy,
    November 8, 2016.

Indignados por el Mural. http://www.facebook.com/Indignadosporelmural, March, 2012.

Lemoyne, James. "In Salvador Village, Can There Be Peace of Mind?" Special to The New York Times.
    March 20, 1987.

Koch, Alexander, Chris Brierley, Mark Maslin, and Simon Lewis. "European colonisation of the Americas
    killed 10% of world population and caused global cooling." *The Conversation*, University College London,
    January 31, 2019. https://theconversation.com/us/topics/central-america-11994?page=2

Martínez Daglio, Manuel, composer and lyricist of "Abriendo Camino." Recorded by La Banda del Sol.
    Unidad, Media Muv Discos, 1971.

Menjívar, Élmer L. and María Luz Nóchez. "Mi dio risa cuando el Arzobispo hablo de un ojo
    mason." Interview with Fernando Llort. El Faro Express, November 6, 2013.

Molina, Rodolfo Francisco, curator. Fernando Llort: abriendo camino: exhibición retrospectiva
    de Fernando Llort, 12 de julio al 19 agosto 2012, Sala Nacional de Exposiciones Salarrué.
    San Salvador: Fundación Fernando Llort.

Morris-Young, Dan. "Memories of Romero" feature series. National Catholic Reporter,
    March 24, 2018.

Nóchez, María Luz. "Adiós al artista omnipresente: la herencia de Fernando Llort." El Faro,
    August 12, 2018.

Raftree, Linda. "On Pueblo and Cathedral, Ruin and Rebuilding." Wait...What? January 3, 2012.
    http://lindaraftree.com/2012/01/03/on-pueblo-and-cathedral-ruin-and-rebuilding.

Sheaffer, Caroline and Donald J. Seiple. "Afflicted with Hope." Embracing El Salvador,
    Outreach ministry of Saint Stephen Evangelical Lutheran Church, New Kingston, PA.
    http://embracingelsalvador.org/fernando.llort.

Silva, Mauricio. "Los Primeros años de Llort." FACTUM Magazine, August 17, 2018. https://www.revistafactum.com/primeros-anios-llort.

Smith, Victoria C., Antonio Costa, and Gerardo Aguirre-Díaz et al. "The Magnitudeand Impact of the 431 CE *Tierra Blanca Joven* Eruption of Ilopango, El Salvador." *Proceedings of the National Academy of Sciences of the United States of America (PNAS)*, v. 117, No. 42.

Personal Interviews

Fernando Llort. San Salvador, El Salvador, August 7, 2018.

Estela Llort Chacón, Fernando's widow. San Salvador, El Salvador, October 21, 2019.

Juan Pablo Llort, Fernando's oldest son. San Salvador, El Salvador, October 24, 2019.

María Cristíne Llort, Fernando's sister. San Salvador, El Salvador, October 24, 2019.

María José Llort, Fernando's daughter. Communications via email.

Mercedes Llort Wise, cousin of Fernando. Communications via Skype: February 18, 2020, April 10, 2020.

Roberto Enrique Burgos, La Palma artist. La Palma, El Salvador, October 25, 2019.

José Anibal Fuentes, San Salvador artist at *El Arbol de Dios*. October 21, 2019.

Julio Medrano, friend of Fernando. San Salvador, El Salvador, October 24, 2019.

TIMELINE OF FERNANDO LLORT'S LIFE

1949	April 7. Fernando Llort born in San Salvador.
1953	Begins first grade at age 4 with special dispensation.
1964	Graduates from high school at age 15 (*del Liceo Salvadoreño*). Studies with painter and ceramics master César Sermeño at *Escuela Nacional de Bellas Artes*.
1965	Studies architecture at the University of El Salvador.
1966	Begins his seminary studies in France.
1968	Graduates with a degree in philosophy and begins his theology courses in Belgium.
1970s	Guerrilla activities and protests grow in El Salvador.
1971	Fernando rejects architecture, returns to San Salvador. Forms "La Banda del Sol," which becomes a popular rock band.
1972	Moves to La Palma, begins art workshops. Meets Estela.
1973	Fernando and Estela get married and work together, helping village artists.
1977	Fernando and Estela establish artists cooperative in La Palma. General Carlos Romero elected president. Persistent violence, death squads. Guerrilla activities intensify.
1980	March 24. Archbishop Óscar Romero assassinated. Beginning of the Civil War.
1980s	Fernando and his family flee from threats to Mexico. Returns to San Salvador, establishes new workshop and classes. His art is featured in museums and exhibits in Central America, Europe, Asia and United States.
1989	Establishes Fernando Llort Foundation to promote Salvadoran arts and provide alternatives to gang violence.

| 1992 | January 16. Signing of *Chapultepec* Peace Accord in Mexico City ends war. |

| 1997 | Commissioned by Archbishop of San Salvador to design and build mural for the restoration of the Metropolitan Cathedral in celebration of peace. |

| 1999 | March. Inauguration of restored Cathedral. |

| 2011 | December. Destruction of Cathedral façade begins. |

| 2012 | Creation of *Abrezo Fraterno* with broken pieces of Mural. |

| 2018 | August 10. Fernando Llort dies at age 69. |

SELECTED HONORS

| 1986 | Exporter's National Prize, handicrafts category. Granted by the Ministry of Foreign Commerce. |

| 1998 | Image Prize. Granted by the Salvadoran Chamber of Tourism. |

| 2003 | Honored as *Hijo Meritísimo* (Distinguished Son) of El Salvador. Granted by the the Legislative Congress of the Republic of El Salvador. |

| 2004 | Ingenuity Prize, paintings category. Granted by the National Centre of Registry. |

| 2008 | Culture Prize, Lic. Antonía Portillo de Galindo. Granted by the Salvadoran American Cultural Centre (CCSA). |

| 2008 | Issue of postage stamps in honor of his contribution to the development of the artisan movement in El Salvador. |

| 2012 | National Prize of Tourism. Hugo Martinez, Salvadoran Minister of Foreign Affairs praised Fernando for "giving the country a symbol that characterizes it and that makes it become a carrier of our national culture." |

| 2013 | El Salvador National Prize of Culture. |

The Author

Although Teddi Ahrens has a professional background in sociology and education, she has been writing since about third grade. Her favorite stories and activities are with children, whether writing about them, reading with them, or creating arts and crafts with them. Her other love is traveling, especially exploring ancient sites wherever she goes and learning about the people and cultures found there. That's how she made the wonderful discovery of Fernando Llort and his art. And that's how she came to write *Painting Joy*.

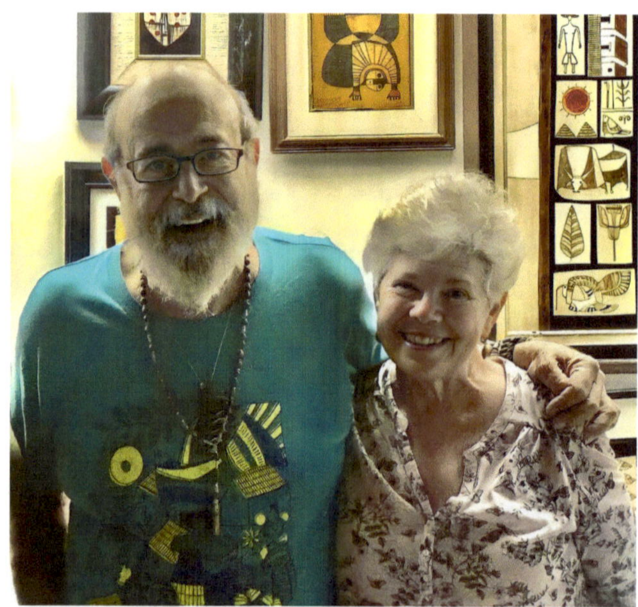

Fernando Llort with the author, August 2018